DAY HIKES IN THE TAOS AREA

by

Kay Matthews

A C E Q U I A   M A D R E

P • R • E • S • S

Box 6 El Valle Route
Chamisal, New Mexico 87521

TABLE OF CONTENTS

SECTION IV. TAOS CANYON

SECTION V. COLUMBINE-HONDO

SECTION VI. WHEELER PEAK

SECTION VII. RED RIVER

SECTION VIII. TRES RITOS

SECTION IX. SANTA BARBARA

INTRODUCTION

Sometimes, as I walk in the mountains, I think of the people who walked here before me and I am amazed. The Native Americans, Spanish and Mexican explorers, and Anglo pioneers who found their way through these rugged mountains to establish trade routes and homes had no trails to guide them, only their spirit, curiosity, and determination. I am thankful that their routes have become my trails, entry into a natural world that remains fresh and new for those of us who make the effort to connect. Every time one hikes a trail it is an adventure, a step into an environment that is both spontaneous and orderly in a way that is largely alien to humans, reared on a man-made order that too often sees itself disconnected from the workings of the natural world. One day an elk will step from the forest canopy, sniff the air, and make a startled leap across the meadow as it detects your presence. Another day you may come to an overlook that reveals itself as it never has before—the sky a sapphire blue, punctuated by clouds perfectly poised above the highest peak.

This book is written for the day hiker, resident or visitor to the Taos area, who wants to enjoy the diverse experience even a relatively short hike offers: respite from the urban world of traffic, rush, and material concerns; a feeling of health and vitality; the opportunity to smell a flower, watch a hawk, or sit under a tree.

All of the trails included in this book are in Carson National Forest, mostly outside the boundaries of the Pecos or Wheeler Peak wilderness areas (wilderness trails are included in my book *Hiking the Wilderness*). I have divided the trails into six sections: (1) Taos Canyon trails, accessed east from the town of Taos along US 64; (2) Columbine-Hondo trails, accessed from NM 150, the Taos Ski Valley Road; (3) Wheeler Peak trails, also accessed from NM 150; (4) Red River Trails, accessed from NM 150 near the town of Red River; (5) Tres Ritos trails, accessed from NM 518 near the town of Tres Ritos; and (6) Santa Barbara Campground trails, near the town of Peñasco. Under the name of each trail are listed the mileage (round-trip), the degree of difficulty (based on elevational gain and mileage), the beginning and ending elevation, applicable maps, and directions to the trailhead. I've tried to make the trail descriptions as clear and precise as possible, hopefully without spoiling all the fun of discovery. Remember, even though a guide book provides you with information about a trail that in turn enables you to hike safely and knowledgeably, to be in the ever-changing mountain environment is always a revelatory experience.

A diverse group of hikers

Section I. General Information

SANGRE DE CRISTO RANGE

Carson National Forest lies in the heart of the Sangre de Cristo mountain range, the eastern-most spur of the great Rocky Mountains extending south from Colorado. The Sangres rise from mesas and plains to mountain peaks over 13,000 feet in elevation. The name, Sangre de Cristo, translates to Blood of Christ in English, and some say the name derives from the killing of the Spanish missionaries by the Pueblo Indians in the 17th century. That image is supported by the historical significance of the Penitente Brotherhood, active in these mountains during the 19th century, who re-enacted the shedding of the "Sangre de Cristo" through self-flagellation.

The Sangre de Cristos have always played an important role in the lives of the diverse peoples who settled the valleys and foothills surrounding the range. They determine weather patterns and ecological divisions and have provided the water, firewood, game, and grazing land necessary for the sustenance of all its people—Native American, Hispanic, and Anglo. Today, while many people remain dependent upon the mountains' resources for their livelihood, others see the Sangres primarily as an oasis of relief for an increasingly urbanized society. And that often creates conflict, when those advocating the mountains' value for recreational and aesthetic purposes fail to appreciate the mountains' historical role in sustaining rural economies. As preservationists fight to preserve old growth and protect endangered species indigenous to these mountains, land-based communities also struggle to maintain a rural economy based on sustainable logging and grazing practices. The two struggles need not be mutually exclusive, as the Sangre de Cristos, with careful management, can provide all things to all people—the gift of water, lumber and wood products, diverse habitat for all creatures, a haven for the human spirit and soul.

MANAGEMENT

The Sangre de Cristo Mountains of north central New Mexico, where all of the following trails are located, are managed by Carson National Forest, one of the larger New Mexico forests encompassing 1,507,000 acres of forest and 330 miles of trails. Because most of the trails described are not in a wilderness area, the lands they cross are managed for the multiple-uses of recreation, timber, mining, grazing, watershed, and wildlife. Also because of their non-wilderness status, these lands are sometimes open to bicycle, snowmobile, and all terrain vehicle (ATV) use, and signs indicating such use are usually placed at trailheads.

As more and more people come to Carson National Forest, conflicts arise over the types of recreation they want to pursue. Hikers may resent the fact that certain trails are open to ATV use, cross-country skiers don't want snowmobilers ruining their track or endangering their lives, and mountain bikers want more attention paid to their sport. The Forest Service has already dealt with these conflicts, to some degree, by designating certain trails and areas of the forest for specific use. The Carson National Forest map, available at the Supervisor's Office in Taos and at the various local ranger stations (addresses are listed below), shows the break down on management areas within the forest with a color-coded system as well as a listing of symbols and travel terms.

Within Carson are 86,193 acres of wilderness lands, managed under the auspices of the 1964 Wilderness Act, which set aside "an area of federal land retaining its primeval character and influence, without permanent improvements or habitation, which is protected and managed so as to preserve its natural condition." Many of the trails in this book are close to or border these wilderness lands (or are in wilderness study areas), and offer the same opportunity for solitude and primitive recreation.

Often the trails described in this book depart from Forest Service developed campgrounds. These trails usually receive the most use and can be hiked during the week or off-season to ensure a more solitary hike. Camping in the Carson is permitted just about anywhere, and many of the trails can be used to access campsites and extend a day hike into an overnight stay. Many of the Carson's most outstanding fishing streams also are accessed by these trails: Rio Pueblo, Rito Angostura, Agua Piedra, Santa

Barbara, Rio Hondo, and Red River.

For maps, information on trail conditions, and any other general information you might desire, you can contact the Supervisor's Office or the local Forest Service district offices listed below.

Supervisor's Office
P. O. Box 558/208 Cruz Alta Road
Taos, NM 87571
(505) 758-6200

Camino Real Ranger District
P. O. Box 68
Peñasco, NM 87553
(505) 587-2255

Questa Ranger District
P. O. Box 110
Questa, NM 87556
(505) 758-6230

WEATHER AND LIFE ZONES

Weather conditions on trails in the Sangre de Cristos can change dramatically in a matter of minutes due to the varied nature of the terrain and dramatic changes in altitude. Hiking the trails of these mountains can be like taking a trip from the Sonoran desert of Mexico to that of the alpine tundra of Canada. Each climate, or life zone, is identified by elevation, exposure, latitude, and prevailing weather patterns. For every 1,000-foot elevation gain, the temperature can decrease 5 degrees.

Some of the hikes included in this book begin in what is called the Upper Sonoran life zone, generally found at 6,500 to 7,500 feet in elevation, a climate hot in the summer while fairly mild in the winter. The sparse vegetation includes the ubiquitous Rocky Mountain juniper and the piñon pine, the decorative chamisa, Apache plume, chokecherry, gambel oak, and the cottonwood and box elder, which usually denote a spring. In the summertime, these Upper Sonoran springs are the first to dry up, so if your hike remains in this life zone, be sure to carry an adequate supply of water (on a day hike you can always carry enough water from home, as opposed to filtering or treating spring water). The array of wildflowers includes the milkvetch and rockcress of springtime, the globemallow, coneflower, and wild buckwheat of fall.

Animals, especially birds and rodents, are abundant in this life zone. While you will probably not see many of them on your hike, this zone is home to pocket mice, Kangaroo rats, prairie dogs, ground squirrels, coyotes, foxes, rattlesnakes, king snakes, lizards, mule deer, mountain lions, and Rocky Mountain bighorn sheep. The latter two species, once hunted to near extinction and reintroduced in several areas of the state, remain low in population and vulnerable to man-made pressures such as habitat intrusion and illegal hunting. Part of a herd of bighorn sheep was recently captured in the Pecos Wilderness and released into the Wheeler Peak Wilderness.

As you enter the Transition life zone (7,599 to 8,200 feet), the piñon pine/juniper vegetation begins to give way to the stately ponderosa pine, easily recognized by the reddish bark of the more mature trees and the distinctive smell of vanilla emanating from the trunk. Here the climate is slightly cooler and wetter than that of the Upper Sonoran. Other trees and bushes include the limber pine (named for its soft, pliant limbs), New Mexico locust, gray oak, mountain mahogany, wild rose, and buckthorn. In the upper reaches of the Transition zone, the aspen and Rocky Mountain maple color fall hiking days yellow and red. In meadows and along stream banks bloom water hemlock, cinquefoil, redosier dogwood, and valerian. Pink phlox, western wallflower, and green gentian (deer's ears) grow in the dry, sandy soil.

Many of the same species of animals found in the Upper Sonoran zone also live in the Transition zone. I've seen rattlesnakes as high as 9,000 feet, and the larger mammal species such as sheep and deer travel through both zones. The magnificent elk is also found wandering through this zone as it migrates from higher to lower elevations following the change of seasons. Here you will see, too, the Abert squirrel with its famous tufted ears, and perhaps an elusive red fox or bobcat.

The Canadian zone, between 8,200 and 10,000 feet, is where you begin to experience the "high country" feeling and is the predominant zone of most of the described hikes. When hiking on trails in this zone you should always come prepared for cooler weather with a jacket, hat, and gloves, as well as rain gear for the thunderstorms that can quickly descend. Thick stands of Douglas fir, white fir, Engelmann spruce, and blue spruce create a sense of the forest primeval. You will also see the ancient bristlecone pine, the oldest of our region, distinguished by its long needles coated with drops of white sap. Mountain meadows are dotted with clusters of aspen and carpeted with larkspur, columbine, fireweed, gentian, osha, geraniums, and bluebells. Here, in summertime, populations of mule deer, an occasional white-tailed deer, Rocky Mountain bighorn sheep, and elk graze. Black bears, the biggest New Mexico carnivores, are still abundant in the Sangre de Cristos. Their signs—scratch marks high up on aspen trees and torn-up trail signs—are common, and I've encountered the backside of a bear turning tail to run at the first sight of me. Beaver dams are evident in some of the mountain streams and lakes, although the creatures themselves, largely nocturnal, are elusive.

The Hudsonian zone is found at 10,000 to 12,500 feet in elevation. The more homogeneous vegetation is exposed to the harsh weather conditions similar to that of the Hudson Bay area of Canada. Here grow the Engelmann spruce, cork bark fir (named for its soft, spongy, cork-like bark), white fir, and aspen. Many of the same wildflowers of the Canadian zone grow here, along with Rocky Mountain iris, primrose, monkshood, and the fairy slipper orchid.

Living among the talus slopes of this region are the sometimes shy, sometimes emboldened marmot and pika. The larger, fat marmots like to sun themselves on rocks during the day while they nibble on grasses and keep an alert eye on hikers. The Rocky Mountain bighorn sheep also love this zone, and while they mostly frequent the lakes of the wilderness areas, you may be lucky enough to see them on one of the hikes that take you near the wilderness.

A few of the hikes in the Wheeler Peak area, and the hike above Serpent Lake, enter the Alpine zone, where the treeline stops at 12,500 feet. Here, weather conditions are so severe that only low growing plants and flowers can survive. New Mexico has only a few peaks this high, and climbing them can be a real challenge. Many wildflowers bloom throughout the summer, though, turning the barren rock and tundra into a carpet of color:

parry primrose, anemone, goldenrod, moss silene, stonecrop, buttercup, and parry gentian proliferate.

TRAILS

All the trails described in the following chapters are accessible to Taos for day hikes and have been arranged in 5 sections according to their geographic locations. Section IV, Taos Canyon, describes those trails closest to Taos, accessed from US 64 east of town in Taos Canyon. Section V, Columbine-Hondo, details those trails northeast of Taos along NM 150, the highway to Taos Ski Valley. Section VI, Wheeler Peak, contains the trails within the Wheeler Peak Wilderness which lead to the state's highest mountain, Wheeler Peak. Section VII, Red River, includes the trails accessed out of the town of Red River, on the north side of the Sangre de Cristo range (many of these trails connect with the Columbine-Hondo section). Section VIII, Tres Ritos, includes the trails southeast of Taos along NM 518, which leads to the towns of Mora and Las Vegas. Section IX, Santa Barbara Campground, describes the trails near Santa Barbara Campground, accessed from the town of Peñasco.

Round-trip mileages for both loop hikes and trails you enter and return the same way, degree of difficulty (based on elevational gain and mileages), and beginning and ending elevations are listed in the headings of each trail. I've listed the applicable forest map for each trail as well as the USGS quadrant map. Explicit directions to the trailhead are also listed in the heading. Included in the main trail descriptions are junctions encountered, views available, flora and fauna you might see, and geologic information. Some of the trails are accompanied by a special section detailing colorful personalities or history associated with the trail. I haven't listed an approximate hiking time as I've found it is too variable, due to a hiker's ability and interest (is this a marathon excursion or leisurely stroll?). All of the trails can be easily hiked in a day, but can easily be turned into a backpack trip by by extending routes.

Many of the trails are in various states of disrepair due to human use, ATV use, pack-animal use, and lack of maintenance by the Forest Service (due to lack of funding and misplaced priorities in spending). Oftentimes, new routes are blazed within a matter of days as detours around fallen logs, washouts, etc., reveal how fragile the landscape is. Try to avoid blazing these new routes yourself or cutting switchbacks which cause erosion. Most forest trails have been laid out to prevent erosion or other kinds of damage to the terrain, so stick to the given trail whenever possible. This may be next to impossible on a rainy day behind a pack train, but try not to create a new trail for others to follow. When you do come across obstacles on the trail, move them if you can, or notify the ranger station when you get back to civilization. Please don't leave cairns (rocks piled up as trail markers) or mark up trees. Again, notify the Forest Service about trail signs that are down or vandalized. Maybe if enough of us complain, more money will be spent on trail maintenance than developed recreation.

Section II. Preparation

It's a good idea to always carry a day pack when heading out for a hike, be it for one mile or ten. In it should be at least one quart of water (two quarts in the summertime), a jacket and rain poncho, something to eat, matches, a map, small first-aid kit, and sunscreen. Each of these items indicates areas of concern that all hikers should consider and plan for.

MAPS

I personally love maps. I like being able to stand on a ridge, look at the map, and pinpoint where I am in the scheme of things. It's good not to be fanatical about it, though, and become so dependent on the map that you forget it's only an aid to outdoor enjoyment, not the focal point. Knowing how to read a map is like knowing the names of wildflowers and birds—knowledge facilitates a larger understanding as well as a better appreciation of detail.

Accompanying each trail is a map showing the general location of the hike, the trailhead, route followed, and geographic features such as mountains, lakes, and streams. Larger and more detailed maps are available at the various Forest Service offices and outdoor stores. Topographic quadrant maps, with elevation lines, are the most detailed, although many of these U.S. Geological Survey maps need to be updated to show the location of new trails or relocated trails. The Carson National Forest map, released in 1991, can be used in conjunction with the topographic maps for the most reliable information. The Pecos Wilderness map and Latir Peak and Wheeler Peak Wilderness map show some of the trails included in this book and are quite detailed, with elevation lines. A new Trails Illustrated map, a joint venture of the Forest Service and Native Sons Adventures, was published in 1993, and designates color-coded (as to degree of difficulty) trail-bike routes as well as hiking and cross-country skiing trails.

Carry your map in a waterproof bag in a convenient location in your pack for easy reference. When you find discrepancies between the trail you are hiking and a corresponding map, mark them down on the map for future reference.

CLOTHING

Choice of clothing depends largely on the weather and type of hiking terrain. Because mountain weather can change dramatically in a relatively short time, I always carry some sort of jacket, as well as rain gear, in my pack. For summer, a good combination is a lined windbreaker, which can both keep you warm and dry in a light rain, and a rain poncho or rainproof jacket (such as Gore-tex) for more severe weather. In the fall, add gloves and a hat to your pack, especially if your hike will take you above 9,000 feet. During the especially rainy month of August, some hikers take along a tarp for sitting out a rainstorm.

Shorts and a T-shirt for summer hiking are usually the most comfortable, but remember that the summer sun is very intense and the atmosphere to filter the sun gets thinner the higher you go. If your skin is sensitive, you may want to wear long plants and a long-sleeved shirt instead. You should always wear sunscreen or a brimmed hat. Take the terrain into account as well when deciding what to wear. If the trail is not well maintained and leads through dense vegetation, wear enough clothing to prevent scrapes and cuts from bushes and branches.

SHOES

Proper footwear is essential for a good hike. If you have to contend with blisters and sore feet, you won't be much interested in beautiful scenery, getting to the top of the mountain, or exploring a new trail.

I almost always wear hiking boots with Vibram soles, but I don't think that has to be a hard-and-fast rule. Modern day running shoes or sneakers with their specially designed soles for jogging work well for hiking if a trail is relatively free of rocks, gullies, and loose gravel, and if the weather is temperate.

High-topped leather hiking boots provide the best support for your feet and the best protection against injury. They are essential in inclement weather and rough terrain. On a trail covered with loose gravel even the best running shoe is rendered almost useless. Walking over rocks and roots and depressions can quickly wear out a pair of feet in sneakers, and the possibility of injury is less with the stronger support of a boot—fewer twisted ankles, bruised heels and toes, and blisters. Be sure to break in a new pair of boots before attempting a five-mile hike, though, or boots won't prevent blisters either. Many of the newer style boots that are a cross between a sneaker and boot and are less heavy than an all-leather boot can be broken in very quickly, and are especially good for day hikes.

No hiking boots will prevent blisters unless you wear the proper socks with them. The best combination is a lightweight liner sock next to the feet with a pair of wool socks or wool-synthetic combination as the outer layer. Research has shown that the synthetic materials such as polypropylene are better for liner socks than cotton, due to their ability to wick—repel—the perspiration from your feet.

WATER

There are numerous springs in the Sangre de Cristos, and many, if not most, of the described hikes follow running streams. It is wise never to depend upon these water sources for drinking water on day hikes, however, for two reasons: 1) some of them periodically dry up; and 2) it is recommended one never drink from mountains springs because of bacterial and viral contaminants. Most contaminants are the result of small rodents in the water source, or the presence of cows and large numbers of people in a riparian area.

On day hikes it is quite easy to carry enough water along in your day pack to avoid dependence on springs or streams. In the summer I carry two quarts of water or herbal tea, freezing the screw-top plastic containers half full the night before, then filling them up in the morning so the ice melts slowly on the hike providing a nice, cool drink. Carry them in an outside pocket in your pack for easy access and so the condensation doesn't get the rest of your pack wet.

If you are in a situation where you are unable to carry all the water you will need (such as backpacking), there are several ways to treat mountain water: mechanical filtration, iodine, chlorine, and boiling.

Boiling is the surest method to kill the three basic types of contaminants: bacteria, viruses, and amoebic cysts. A minute boil (three or four minutes at higher elevations) will kill Giardia lamblia, the most pernicious of the intestinal parasites, and 10 minutes kills other bacteria and viruses. Several drawbacks to boiling are the time it takes to boil and cool your water supply and the amount of fuel that has to be carried and consumed.

Mechanical filtration, with pumps that cost anywhere from $25 to $200, guards against Giardia, as the parasite cannot get through the filter, but do allow the smaller viruses through. Contracting a virus like hepatitis is unlikely, however. A recent study has resulted in some dispute as to the reliability of the filter even against Giardia (there is evidence the cysts can survive in the filter), and researchers recommend that you buy the more expensive pumps that have pre-filters or filters that can be cleaned after each use. Some pumps are now made with a silver lining that eliminates bacterial growth in the filter. If you do use the less expensive mechanical pumps, be sure to replace the filter as soon as it begins to clog and look dirty (the filters come with recommended usage capacity as well as tips on storage and cleaning). With any mechanical filter it's a good idea to collect your water in a pot, let it stand for the debris to settle, and then filter.

While chlorine kills bacteria and viruses, it has been determined that Giardia has a resistance to it. Consequently, the chlorine tablets sold in outdoor stores labeled Halozone are not adequate to decontaminate the water. Iodine is the more effective chemical and is sold in the stores as Potable Agua (hyperiodide), which comes in tablets, or iodine crystals, and must be measured. Add one tablet to a quart of water (two if the water is especially dirty) with the lid securely fastened, for at least 20 minutes. Both chlorine and iodine have an unpleasant taste, which makes them less desirable methods of purification.

FOOD

For a day hike, you should pack a good lunch and some snacks, and it's always a good idea to carry more than enough food in case your hike takes longer than anticipated, or an emergency occurs.

Items like cheese, sliced turkey, and crackers provide an alternative to sandwiches. Try to avoid salty foods, or excessively sweet foods, as they tend to make you thirsty. Fruit is always a good item (pack it in a plastic container so it doesn't get squashed) because it provides both energy and liquid. Cut-up vegetables are also easy to carry and provide nourishment. For snacks, high energy bars or dried fruit weigh less than trail mix or "gorp," although on a day hike you don't have to worry too much about extra weight. Try to make your lunches interesting, filling yet nutritious, and easy to pack.

MISCELLANEOUS EQUIPMENT

SUNSCREEN

It's a good idea to always wear sunscreen when hiking, especially at high elevations where the sun's rays can do the most damage. Apply the sunscreen before you leave home (to any exposed skin, especially the top of your head if you lack much hair) and reapply periodically during the day. A brand rated 15 or higher is adequate.

SUNGLASSES

My eyes get very tired when hiking in bright sunshine if I don't wear sunglasses. The kind that protect your eyes from ultraviolet rays are a good investment (and will come in handy for skiing as well).

INSECT REPELLENT

I don't know if anyone has ever researched why some people are more tasty to insects—especially mosquitoes—than others, but if you are one of the unlucky ones be sure to carry insect repellent along on your hikes. If your hike is through a riparian area, or the weather is humid, the bugs can be unmerciful (although usually if you keep moving it's easier to avoid getting eaten). Commercial repellents are usually repellent to you as well (they employ unpleasant smelling chemicals), so you may want to try some herbal repellents or rub garlic on your skin, which has proven effective.

COMPASS

It's always a good idea to take along a compass as part of your emergency kit and to know how to use it. Detailed instructions are usually included in a compass package, and it's fun to learn how to take bearings which will provide a safeguard against getting lost.

POCKET KNIFE

A good Swiss army knife serves many needs that may arise—carving, eating, and first aid.

MATCHES

As part of an emergency kit take along matches, even on a day hike. Pack kitchen matches in a waterproof container or ziplock bag.

FIRST AID KIT

A small first-aid kit is also an indispensable part of your emergency kit. With careful planning it's rare that a hiker risks serious injury on a day hike, but there's always the possibility that minor cuts, blisters, or bruises may occur.

Moleskin (or second skin) is a must. Even the most broken-in boots in the world can raise a blister on a long, arduous hike, so it's wise to prevent possible blisters by applying moleskin to sensitive areas—across the back of the heel or along the side of the big toe. Or you can wait until a spot becomes slightly irritated and then apply the moleskin. Just don't wait until the blister appears, because then even moleskin won't protect you from the pain.

Include a sampling of bandaids in your kit. Take along a dozen or so regular size bandaids, a small package of sterile pads with adhesive tape, and an ace bandage or special knee bandage. The latter is particularly important if you have weak knees that bother you on descents.

I always include some kind of pain reliever, such as ibuprofen, in anticipation of headaches (which can easily occur on long, hot hikes), sore muscles, or to ease the pain of injuries. If you are on medication for some ailment, be sure and take it along, too.

Section III. Safety

EMERGENCIES

Many agencies and authorities say that you should never hike alone. I can understand why that advice is given, but I cannot say that I always follow it. It limits your sense of freedom and stands between you and experiences that you may want to have on your own. If I do decide to to hike alone, though, I adhere to a cardinal rule: I always tell someone where I am hiking and when I expect to return. Then, if I don't show up within a reasonable period of time, the proper authorities can be notified.

All missing hikers should be reported to the New Mexico State Police, who will coordinate the search utilizing highly skilled search-and-rescue teams, the Forest Service, the county sheriff's department, or whomever else they need.

If you do decide to hike alone, be sure to take along your emergency kit that includes a compass, matches, and your first-aid equipment. Small cuts, bruises, and abrasions can be treated on the trail to help prevent infection until further treatment is available. Hikers often ask me if a snakebite kit should be included in the first-aid equipment. My advice is no: According to the American Red Cross, an incision made to suck the venom should only be administered as a last resort, when there is no medical help nearby and the victim is suffering respiration problems. It is very unlikely that hikers will encounter rattlesnakes in these Carson National Forest hikes.

GETTING LOST

With this book in your pack you won't *ever* get lost, of course, but if for some strange reason you do, here are some things to remember. Once you are aware that you are not on the trail, stop immediately and regroup. Try to recall how far back you may have taken a wrong turn or lost the trail, then try and back track to that point. You may be able to retrace your footprints in soft or wet dirt. A compass will keep you pointed in the right direction as indicated by your map. Read your map carefully to identify any landmarks that may help you find where you are in relation to the trail. If you cannot find the trail, but feel confident from the reading of your map that you know approximately where you are and the directions that correspond with the map, you can continue on course to your destination or return to the area of the trailhead. Because so many of the described hikes follow canyons and streams, even if you momentarily loose the trail, by staying in the canyon you will eventually find it again. Another thing to look for when you are unsure of a route are the old Forest Service blazes on trees, usually rectangular cuts carved into the bark about shoulder high.

If you become hopelessly lost, or are injured and unable to hike, sit down and wait for someone to find you (start blowing a whistle if you have brought one). If you have notified someone at home of where you planned to hike, the search-and-rescue team will find you fast. Don't panic, stay put, and make a shelter against the weather if night is approaching. This can be against some rocks, next to a large fallen log or base of a tree, out of the wind and close to the ground. You can keep a small fire going with evergreen needles and sticks if you have to stay out during the night. Any extra food you've brought along should be stretched out over the night to replenish your energy stores.

HYPOTHERMIA

Hypothermia is the lowering of the inner body core temperature due to cold, windy, or wet conditions. Symptoms include shivering, fatigue, disorientation, numbness, slow pulse, blue lips, and slurred speed. If not treated immediately the body temperature can descend irreversibly. Treatment includes taking the victim to shelter, removing wet clothing and warming with a fire, sleeping bag, body heat, or hot bath. Although it is unlikely that a well-prepared hiker will ever have to deal with hypothermia, you should know its symptoms and, more importantly, how to prevent and treat it. Know your hiking limitations (and those of your companions), and don't attempt trips that may be too taxing for your endurance level. If you are attempting an ascent into alpine country and a storm is brewing, consider abandoning your goal and staying at a lower elevation to avoid extreme cold, moisture, or lightening. If you are caught in a rainstorm—or snowstorm—stop and put on your rain gear or head back to the trailhead early before you get wet and cold.

ALTITUDE SICKNESS

This usually occurs above 7,000 feet and is characterized by dizziness, headache, shortness of breath, lack of energy, and nausea. If you begin to feel any of these symptoms, stop, rest, drink fluids, eat some high-energy food, and return to lower elevations. The best prevention is to be sure you're in good physical condition and somewhat acclimated to the climate and altitude where you will be hiking. That's not always possible when you're climbing Wheeler Peak or some other 13,000-foot peak—and you'll find that you'll almost always experience a certain amount of shortness of breath and light-headedness—but you can accomplish the hike if you're adequately prepared.

PHYSICAL CONDITIONING

If you are in reasonable physical shape, a 5-to- 10 mile hike is a wonderful way to get out into the woods and get some exercise as well. The best preparation for a good hike is year-round physical activity, such as swimming, cross-country skiing, bike riding, jogging, etc. At least 20 minutes of exercise three to five times a week to get your cardiovascular system going should be a regular activity. If you like to avoid spas and exercise classes, where exercise for beauty sometimes overshadows exercise for health and enjoyment, achieve your conditioning by playing basketball or racquetball, jogging around the park a few times, or practicing with your kid's soccer team.

FIRE RESTRICTIONS

During critical parts of the summer Carson National Forest may be put under fire restrictions because of dry weather and potential fire hazard. Restrictions can prohibit smoking and camp-fires or mandate a total closure of the forest. Check with the local ranger district to see what, if any, restrictions are in effect. For fire prevention and environmental reasons, the Forest Service requests that hikers and campers refrain from building campfires altogether except in designated areas. Instead, a gas backpacking stove for cooking is recommended.

HIKING ETIQUETTE

Please make sure that your visit to the forest is a "no-trace visit," i.e., that you leave no evidence of your presence—litter, ground disturbance, campfire—and that you take nothing with you—wildflowers, tree seedlings or branches, or any other forest product.

Dogs should be kept on a leash in heavy use areas and under verbal command out on the trail. Train your dog to stay with you and be aware of its limitations before taking it on a long hike. Summer temperatures often turn the lower trails into hotbeds on a dog's tender paws, and you must be willing to carry an adequate water supply for your friend if there's not enough water along the route. If you have hopes of viewing wildlife, it's best to leave your dog at home.

The summer I worked as a Forest Service patrol in the Sandia Mountains near Albuquerque I had to administer first-aid to a hiker who had been hit by a rock thrown down from the top of the mountain. Deny the urge to see your rock fly through space; there are hikers, campers, and rock climbers all over the mountains who want to enjoy an outdoor experience without getting clunked by flying rocks.

When hiking on trails used by horses, mountain bikes, or ATVs, get off the trail and let them pass, for your own safety as well as theirs.

The wildlife viewing us

MAP LEGEND

Trail	– – – –
Intermittent stream	▬ ·· ▬ ··
Dirt road	══════
Paved road	▬▬▬▬▬
Picnic or campground	▶
Peak	▲
Spring	٩

ABBREVIATIONS

CG:	campground
ft:	feet
FR:	national forest road
FT:	national forest trail
Mt:	mountain
NM:	New Mexico highway
Spr:	spring
US:	U.S. highway

Section IV. Taos Canyon

These are the hikes closest to Taos, accessed by U.S. 64, which leads east to Eagle Nest and Angel Fire. Many of them begin in the lower elevation piñon/juniper country but lead up to the high country of 10,000 feet. They are also popular mountain bike trails as well, so be careful. Mileages are given from the junction of NM 68 in Taos, but if you use the NM 585 bypass to access them, I have given the mileages from the forest boundary as well.

DEVISADERO LOOP #108

Length: 6 miles round trip
Degree of Difficulty: Moderate
Elevation: 7,200-8,300 feet
Maps: Trails Illustrated Carson National Forest; USGS Palo Flechado Pass
Finding the Trailhead: The trail is located on US 64 2.8 miles from the junction of 64 and NM 68, across the highway from El Nogal Picnic Ground (just beyond the forest boundary). There is room to park in the picnic ground.

A hike close to Taos, Devisadero Peak is best hiked in the spring or fall because of its low elevation. It's a relatively easy loop hike to the top of Devisadero Peak and back. The first part of the trail climbs rather steeply up rocky terrain through piñon/juniper vegetation. There's a sign with the trail name and number a short distance up the trail. At the power line the trail turns east, circles around the power easement, then crosses under the wires. Leaving the wires, the trail switchbacks up the south side of Devisadero Peak one half mile to a sign that indicates the return of the loop trail. To the right is the closest route to the top of the peak; to the left is the return trail from the back side of the peak. Follow the arrow right (east).

Mark and Max at the Devisadero trailhead

The trail continues climbing, periodically leveling out, to a sign which indicates the 1967 Vinatera burn visible across the canyon. It's a little over 2 miles to the top of the peak, where a sign gives the elevation: 8,304 feet. From here you can see north to Taos Mountain and the Wheeler Peak ridge.

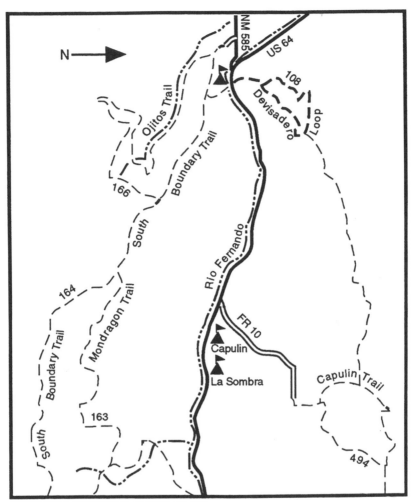

DEVISADERO LOOP #108

You can return the way you came for a shorter hike or follow the continuation of Trail #108 down the north side of the peak and back around to the loop junction. The return leg is a little longer, at about 3 miles in length. From the top of the peak, the trail quickly descends around the east side of the peak to the north side, where the vegetation changes from piñon/juniper to spruce and fir in the colder, north-side climate. Views extend north to Taos Pueblo and Taos Mountain. The trail switchbacks east and west down the north side to a sign which indicates the junction with the North Boundary Trail, which connects Devisadero Trail with the existing Capulin Trail in Capulin Canyon. Stay to the left (west) on Devisadero Trail, which continues downhill along the north side. After about a mile, the trail turns south, along the west side of the peak, with views of Taos and on to the Taos llano.

Back in more exposed piñon/juniper country, the trail skirts the head of five or six small canyons as it crosses several ridges back towards the trailhead. There are a few short uphill sections before the trail crosses the last ridge and completes the loop at the sign a half mile from the trailhead. Continue downhill back to the highway and your car.

SOUTH BOUNDARY TRAIL #164 (to Mondragon Canyon)

Length: 7 miles round trip
Degree of Difficulty: Moderate
Elevation: 7,200-10,000 feet
Maps: Trails Illustrated, Carson National Forest; USGS Osha Mountain
Finding the Trailhead: The trail is located on US 64 2.8 miles from the junction of 64 and NM 68 in Taos (just beyond the forest boundary). Park in El Nogal Picnic Ground and cross over the foot bridge at the west end of the picnic ground. A sign tells you this is a multi-purpose trail utilized by hikers, mountain bikers, and horseback riders.

This is a good hike to take in the spring, before the snows have melted on the higher elevation trails. You can hike as far as the snowline, or to Bear Springs and the junction with Mondragon Canyon Trail #163. Strong hikers might want to make arrangements to leave a car at the Mondragon Canyon trailhead on US 64 and and use this trail as a return route rather than backtracking on South Boundary Trail.

Follow the trail a short distance southwest to the junction with a short trail heading left (east), an easy route that leads to the next

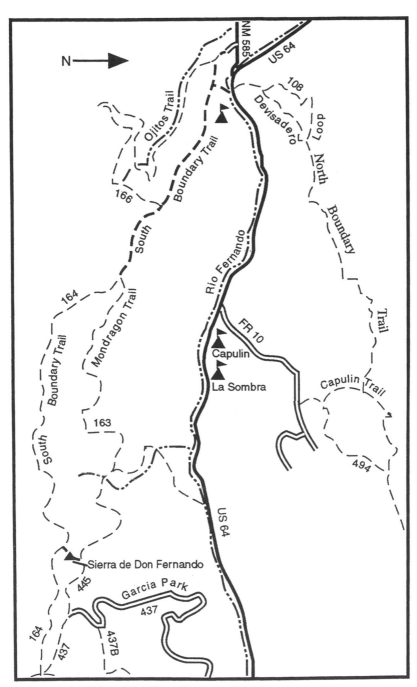

SOUTH BOUNDARY TRAIL #164

picnic ground on US 64. South Boundary Trail continues to the right (west) to a caution sign on a tree (a spur trail leads right, along the river; stay to the left, uphill).

This part of South Boundary Trail climbs about a half mile to the southwest, with several switchbacks near the top, to a junction where it heads both left (east) and right (west).To the west, the trail leads about one half mile to the junction with Ojitos Trail, a 12 mile bike trail that loops around to the south and ties in with South Boundary Trail farther east. To the east, our route, South Boundary Trail continues all the way to Garcia Park (15 miles).

Follow South Boundary Trail to the east as it climbs uphill through the piñon/juniper vegetation; you can see Taos behind you. You'll come to another caution sign on the backside of a tree, where the trail turns to the southeast. In the spring, the fragrant mock orange blooms alongside the trail, along with the showy western wallflower. The trail soon turns to the northeast; watch for a spur trail that leads to a campsite on the edge of the ridge. The main trail continues east, climbing into the next elevation zone, where it levels out under ponderosa pines (smell the reddish bark of these trees for a whiff of vanilla). The trail is on the side of the ridge here, and great views of Taos Mountain and the Wheeler Peak ridge are off to the left.

The trail soon starts climbing again into spruce-fir vegetation, where columbines and clematis line the path. Views extend all the way from Taos to Wheeler Peak. You'll soon come to the junction with Ojitos Trail, a road-like path to the right (there is also a turn to the left). Continue straight ahead along South Boundary Trail. A short climb takes you into open aspen country, where the trail levels out. The trail continues through thick spruce-fir vegetation for a little less than a mile to Bear Springs, which is piped into a wildlife tank next to the trail. A short distance later is the junction with Mondragon Canyon Trail, which heads left (north) 8 miles back down to US 64 (there is a spur trail to the right as well).

CAPULIN TRAIL #494

Length: 7 miles round trip
Degree of Difficulty: Moderate
Elevation: 8,600-9,700 feet
Maps: Trails Illustrated Carson National Forest; USGS Palo Flechado Pass
Finding the Trailhead: Follow US 64 east 6.7 miles from the junction of NM 68 in Taos to FR 10 (4 miles from the forest boundary). The sign here says Shadow Mountain. Follow FR 10 for 1.4 miles to the throw-down camp area. The trail begins across the road from the campground.

On the map this route is shown as a loop hike; however, the return part of the loop is overgrown and not well marked, so most hikers will probably want to return via the same route. Follow the trail leading north into the forest, across several birms, then bear left until you come to an old logging road. This road heads northwest along an easy route lined with mountain mahogany and gambel oak. After about 3/4 mile you'll come to a junction (with a signless post): Turn right (northeast), and the trail gradually climbs through ponderosa pine to spruce-fir vegetation. After awhile, the trail levels out and provides views of Taos Canyon.

It soon climbs again and turns more directly north, providing views west to Taos. As it turns back to the northeast, you can see Taos Mountain and the Wheeler Peak ridge. A culvert under the road indicates a spring, and not far beyond here is the Taos Pueblo boundary, where North Boundary Trail junctions with Capulin Trail. Both trails follow the boundary northwest around the head of a canyon and continue west, then circle another canyon to the northwest. As it turns southwest, you can see the Truchas Peaks to the south. Wild iris, evening primrose, and lupine grow all along the route.

The road appears to dead end, but there is a rather obscure route that continues southwest another mile back to the lower part of the trail, just above the signless post.

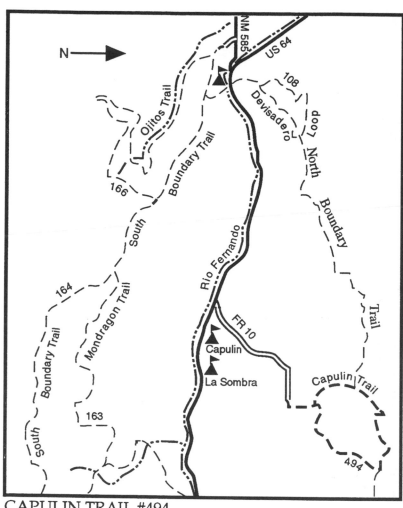

CAPULIN TRAIL #494

SOUTH BOUNDARY TRAIL #164—FOREST ROAD
437 TO PARADISE PARK

Length: 3 miles round trip
Degree of Difficulty: Easy
Elevation: 10,000 feet
Maps: Trails Illustrated Carson National Forest; USGS Osha Mountain
Finding the Trailhead: Take US 64 east from the junction of NM 68 in Taos for 13.2 miles to FR 437, the turn to Valle Escondido (10.5 miles from the forest boundary). Drive .4 miles to the right-turn continuation of FR 437 (the sign says Garcia Park 7 miles, Rio Chiquito 10 miles). This all-weather road leads 6.8 miles to Garcia Park and the junction with Trail 164. Look for trails signs to the left, near a parking pull-off, and leave your car here (before you get to the Garcia Park sign). The road doesn't require a four-wheel drive, but a truck or sports vehicle can better negotiate the ruts and rocks.

This is the middle of South Boundary Trail's 22 mile length. To the east the trail is designated open to ATVs and snowmobiles; our route to the west is restricted to hiking and horseback riding. The route west connects to Trail 164's western trailhead at El Nogal Picnic Ground. This short hike leads to the top of Sierra de don Fernando at Paradise Park. Garcia Park is a popular camping site along FR 437.

Cross the road west towards the meadow at Garcia Park and look across the meadow until you find the steel post with Trail 164 on it, and an arrow pointing west (near the road sign that says Garcia Park). Just beyond this sign is another one with pictures of a hiker and horseback rider. The trail continues west and becomes a jeep road; follow the road through the fence and up to another sign—ATVs prohibited—just as you leave the meadow and enter the trees.

The trail is a gradual uphill climb through mixed conifer forest; several stacked woodpiles indicate the route. In another small meadow the trail passes through a fence and picks up another old road; bear west along the road through the meadow full of hare-bells. Back in the trees, a sign on an aspen shows that the trail bears southwest (left). A quarter mile walk brings you to another junction; again bear left through the meadow.

The trail soon reaches the junction with a section of FR 445. A trail marker in the trees across the road indicates the continuation of Trail 164. The road you cross is a spur of FR 445 which dead-ends to your left and continues both east and west to your right. If you take a short detour to the left you'll get a view of the mountains stretching south, and you might find some of the largest strawberries I've ever encountered—if it's near the end of July.

Continue on the trail through the woods. It's not far to the next junction with FR 445: This is the same road you just passed in its continuation west, and it now follows the same route as FT 164. This is the end of our hike; you can climb to the top of Sierra de don Fernando, just to the east, for a panoramic view. If you choose to follow Trail 164 west it continues through Mondragon Canyon and on to El Nogal Campground. If you follow FR 445 to the right you soon come to the junction of the Mondragon Canyon spur road that leads back down to Taos Canyon.

Remember on your return route to bear right at junctions (be sure to cross the first meadow all the way through to the junction right, as another old road comes into the meadow before this junction and may confuse you).

JICARITA TRAIL #121

Length: 4 miles round trip
Degree of Difficulty: Easy
Elevation: 9,600-10,300 feet
Maps: Trails Illustrated Carson National Forest; USGS Osha Mountain
Finding the Trailhead: Take US 64 east from the junction of NM 68 in Taos for 13.2 miles to FR 437, the turn to Valle Escondido (10.5 miles from the forest boundary). Drive .4 miles to the right-turn continuation of FR 437 (the sign says Garcia Park 7 miles, Rio Chiquito 10 miles). This all-weather road leads 7.2 miles to the junction with FR 438 in Garcia Park. Turn left on 438 (south) and follow it 4.1 miles to the Jicarita trailhead at the Rio Chiquito. There is a parking pull-off right at the signless post marking the trail.

This is a lovely riparian hike along the Rio Chiquito to a ridge overlooking Angel Fire, where FR 153 connects to FR 76. The trail

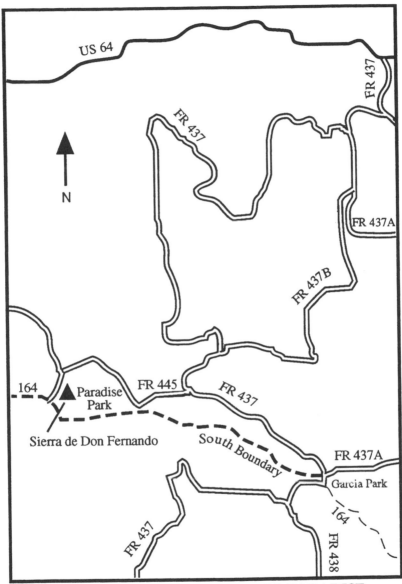

SOUTH BOUNDARY TRAIL #164 TO PARADISE
PARK

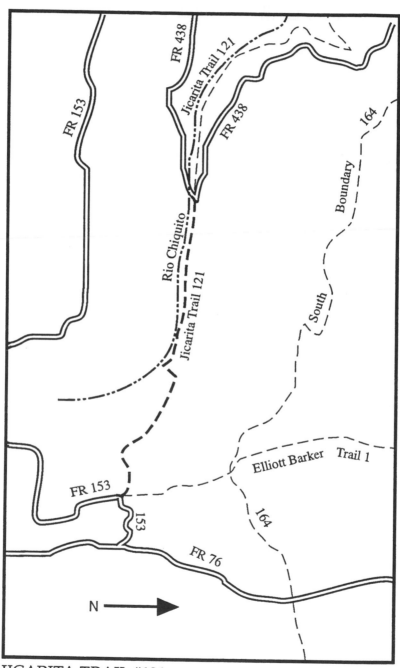

JICARITA TRAIL #121

is somewhat hard to follow, as it doesn't get much use, but cairns and birms along the old logging road mark the route.

Follow the trail east along the north side of the Rio Chiquito (stay next to the river rather than climbing to the old road above the trail sign). The route passes through numerous meadows where you must look for the trail as it reenters the trees. There is much beaver activity in the river, and the area is popular with fishermen. It's an easy mile-climb through stands of diverse forest, including some of the largest firs I've ever seen in the southwest.

A trail sign and cairn indicate a turn right (south) across a tributary of the Rio Chiquito. Here you pick up an old logging road that has been birmed; follow it to a meadow where you'll see the remains of an old cabin. The meadow is full of the beautiful tulip gentian and elephant head. Continue south through the meadow alongside the Rio Chiquito for less than half a mile to a sharp switchback to the left (east); here the trail leaves the Rio Chiquito and climbs along the old birmed road to Jaracita Park. This is the steepest section of the trail ; the terrain levels out as the trail parallels the open meadow of the park. It is quite lush here, with numerous species of mushrooms growing alongside the water-loving monkey flower and monkshood. The trail continues to the junction of FR 153, where a large clearcut affords an incredible view north to the Wheeler Peak area and east to Angel Fire. Climb the clearcut ridge for the views, but be careful to look for the cairn that marks the route back into the trees.

NORTH BOUNDARY TRAIL—LA JARA CANYON

Length: Variable mileage, 23 miles total length
Degree of Difficulty: Moderate
Elevation: 9,200-8,300 feet
Maps: Trails Illustrated Carson National Forest; USGS Palo Flechado Pass
Finding the Trailhead: Take US 64 17.7 miles from the junction of 64 and NM 68 to Forest Road 5, just before the switchback which leads up to Palo Flechado Pass (15 miles from the forest boundary). Follow this forest road for almost two miles to a parking pull-off where the road divides. You need a relatively high-clearance vehicle to negotiate the pot holes.

North Boundary Trail traverses the boundary ridge between Carson National Forest and Taos Pueblo, from La Jara Canyon to Devisadero Peak. Please respect the boundary and do not cross onto Pueblo land. The entire length of the trail is approximately 23 miles; I have included this day-hike description of the upper portion of the trail. North Boundary Trail ties in with Capulin Trail (or Shadow Mountain Ranch) and Devisadero Trail, at its western terminus.

Leave your car where the road divides and follow the left fork a short way uphill until you see another primitive road to the left. Follow this road up a relatively steep climb, staying to the right at the next fork. Keep climbing to the junction with the boundary fence, where the road turns west (left), our route. To the right a narrow trail leads downhill to the La Jara Canyon Road. Over your shoulder you can catch glimpses east to the high peaks above the Moreno Valley.

The trail follows the general direction of the fenceline the entire route. The road eventually disappears, and after the initial climb the route levels out. The trail swings around to the southwest, where an additional fence heads north across Pueblo land. It then descends into the first of many small auxiliary canyons. Through the mixed-conifer vegetation you can just see east to the Angel Fire Ski Area. While the views are mostly obscured by the trees, there are abundant wildflowers and wildlife on this trail. The last time I hiked this route I noticed a lot of elk droppings alongside the fence; soon I encountered a herd of elk in a forest meadow. I also flushed a couple of grouse along the way. Flowers include

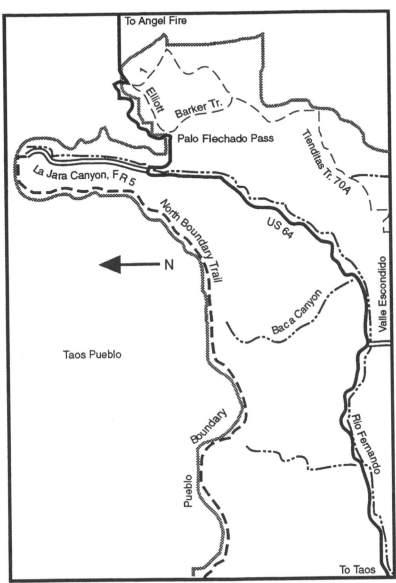

To Angel Fire

Elliott

Barker Tr.

Palo Flechado Pass

Tiendtias Tr. 70A

La Jara Canyon, FR 5

North Boundary Trail

US 64

N

Baca Canyon

Valle Escondido

Taos Pueblo

Boundary

Rio Fernando

Pueblo

To Taos

NORTH BOUNDARY TRAIL

38

Indian paintbrush, death camus, harebell, and strawberries. If you travel as far as Baca Canyon, watch for the trail as it intersects a road and follows it left, away from the fence, down into the canyon.

Follow the trail as far as you like before retracing your steps back the same way.

ELLIOTT BARKER TRAIL #1
Length: 6 miles round trip
Degree of Difficulty: Easy to moderate
Elevation: 9,000-9,700 feet
Maps: Trails Illustrated Carson National Forest; USGS Palo Flechado Pass
Finding the Trailhead: Take US 64 18.6 miles from the junction of 64 and NM 68 to Flechado Pass (15.9 miles from the forest boundary). Park your car at the large pull-off on the north side of the pass. The trail begins directly across the road at the walk-through gate.

A Man of all Trades

This trail is named for Elliott Barker: rancher, hunter, and Forest Service ranger from an illustrious New Mexico family which settled in Sapello Canyon above Las Vegas in 1889. Seven members of the family have written their autobiographies, and Omar Barker, Elliott's brother, was a well-known western writer with poems, short stories, articles, and one novel to his credit. Elliott Barker was intimately familiar with the Pecos Wilderness, where he went on extensive horse trips with his family and patrolled as district Forest Service ranger. He later served on the Carson National Forest as ranger, land examiner, deputy supervisor, forest supervisor, and state game warden. In his position as warden, Barker was instrumental in the decision to have the orphaned bear cub found in the 1950 Capitan forest fire designated as the official Forest Service symbol for fire prevention. Barker also authored several books. *Beatty's Cabin* is a collection of stories of the Pecos high country centering around the infamous George Beatty, miner and adventurer whose cabin in the Pecos Wilderness Barker first visited when he was a 10-year-old boy. He also wrote *When the*

Elliott Barker

Dogs Bark 'Treed', based on Barker's experiences as game manager of the 360,000 acre Vermejo Park.

In his book *Beatty's Cabin* Barker gives a brief account of how the national forests came into being. He quotes Gifford Pinchot, the first United States Forester: "In 1891, the most important legislation in the history of forestry in America slipped through Congress without question and without debate. It was an amendment to the Act of March 3, 1891, 'For the Repeal of the Timber and-Stone Act and for other Purposes,' and it authorized creation of Forest Reserves. This was the beginning and the basis of our whole National Forest System." The reason this act slipped through Congress was due to the fact that Gifford Pinchot had long been lobbying to end the exploitation of the country's forest lands by the extractive industries.

When these forest reserves were created, however, there was no provision made for their administration, management, and use: the areas were merely withdrawn from every kind of use, including timbering, grazing, mining, and technically, recreation. It was not until 1897 that legislation was finally passed which gave the Secretary of the Interior authority to open them to regulated use and the practice of forestry. Even though the Division of Forestry, within the Department of Agriculture, was created in 1880, the forest reserves remained under the control of the intensely political Department of the Interior for seven more years. Battles were waged over the management of the reserves by not only mining, grazing and timbering interests, but also by factions reflecting two different preservationist policies: preservation of esthetic resources or preservation for limited commodity resource production. Finally, in February of 1905, during Theodore Roosevelt's administration, the reserves were transferred to the Department of Agriculture. "President Roosevelt, undoubtedly, made the greatest contribution to conservation of natural resources of any man who ever lived. During his administration, 1902 to 1909, the area within forest reserve boundaries increased from 62,354,965 acres to 194,505,325 acres," Barker says. The reserves were soon renamed "national forests," and in 1905, the Bureau of Forestry became the Forest Service. Barker again quotes Pinchot: "We had the power as we had the duty, to protect the Reserves for the use of the people, and that meant stepping on the toes of the biggest interests of the West. From that time on, it was fight, fight, fight,

fight. We who took over the Forest Reserves preferred the small man before the big man because his need was greater . . . . The Forest Service was the first government organization not only to assert that the small man had the first right to the natural resources of the West, but actually to make it stick. Better help a poor man make a living for his family than help a rich man get richer still. That was our battle cry and our rule of life." Unfortunately, the battles didn't end there: We are still fighting the "big man's" exploitation of the forests in northern New Mexico today.

The Hike

Elliott Barker Trail extends along the rim of the Moreno Valley from Palo Flechado Pass on US 64 south to Osha Mountain. A hiking group from the Angel Fire area has worked extensively on this trail system, and the loop route described below has been blazed by the group. The described 6-mile loop both begins and ends at Palo Flechado Pass.

Follow the trail to the right (southwest) to begin the loop. A snowmobile blaze on a tree marks the route, which is subsequently blazed with arrows on posts in the ground. The route travels through ponderosa pine with a thick undergrowth of bushy cinquefoil, wild iris (in the spring), and sebadillosos. The trail follows the path of an old road and climbs to the top of the ridge, where you'll pass through a fence to views that extend east to the Moreno Valley.

Keep bearing right at the junction with an old road to the left, and you can see the town of Angel Fire and the ski area off in the valley. Soon you'll come to a junction where the trail branches right and left: to the left (north) is the continuation of Elliott Barker Trail back to Palo Flechado Pass; to the right (south), Elliott Barker Trail continues on its 6-mile route to Osha Mountain. Before turning left on the loop back to the trailhead, you might want to continue south on Elliott Barker as far as Apache Pass for some good views and a little extra mileage to your hike.

Turn right at the junction and follow the trail through a large meadow full of more bushy cinquefoil and wild iris, with a view to Taos Mountain. A gate leads through the fence to a sign: Palo Flechado Pass, 3 miles back along the loop trail; OK Canyon and

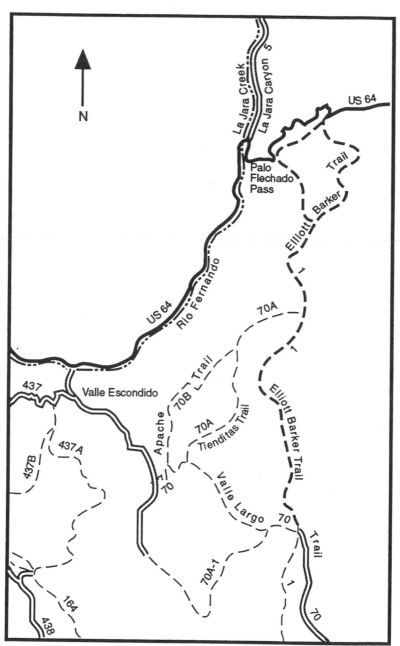

ELLIOTT BARKER TRAIL #1

US 64, 1³/4 miles west; and Apache Pass, 1¹/4 miles south. Continue south through the meadow and up into the trees. The trail soon levels out in an area of dying ponderosas (looks like an old burn). From here you can see west to the Garcia Park area before the trail heads downhill to Apache Pass at the powerline.

Turn left and follow the powerline to the fence where you can see the town of Angel Fire down in the valley. A sign with a picture of hikers indicates the continuation of Elliott Barker Trail south; the junction with Tienditas Trail #70A is just a few feet down the trail. Tienditas Trail, an old four-wheel drive route, leads southwest to the Valle Escondido Road near Garcia Park (2.3 miles from US 64).

Our route turns back north along Elliott Barker Trail to the continuation of the loop back to Palo Flechado Pass. Once you have retraced your steps back through the meadow, continue straight along the trail, passing the route we used coming to the meadow. There are almost constant views of the Moreno Valley and Angel Fire to your right (east) as the trail descends to the northeast along an old road. There are also several spectacular views of the Wheeler Peak ridge up ahead of you to the north. There are several signs indicating this is Elliott Barker Trail, and several arrows on trees keep you on the main road as various spur routes intersect the road.

After several miles you'll come to another sign with a picture of hikers on it; the trail turns left (west) here, up into the trees (the road you are on continues straight ahead for less than ¹/4 mile to a gate at US 64). Follow the trail through the trees to another junction. This is the trail leading from a second trailhead on US 64, just to your right (there is a trail sign at this trailhead giving various mileages along Elliott Barker Trail). Turn left (south), and the loop continues southwest, paralleling the highway.

The trail climbs up through a meadow to a man-made pond. To your right (west), you'll see a post with an arrow indicating the route along an old road. This route climbs a little less than a mile back to the trailhead at Palo Flechado Pass (you'll be able to hear the cars on the highway all along the trail).

Section V. Columbine-Hondo

The Columbine-Hondo area, encompassing 43,000 acres, is actually a proposed wilderness offering the same kinds of high-country experiences as the neighboring Wheeler Peak Wilderness. The trails leading north along NM 150—Yerba Canyon, Manzanita Canyon, and Italianos—lead to the higher trails within the Columbine-Hondo area—Lobo Peak, Long Canyon and Gold Hill. In turn, these trails connect with the hikes described in the Red River section.

The Columbine-Hondo Proposed Wilderness is part of the RARE II wilderness study plan made in the 1980s: The Forest Service completed the study of this area only recently and has made its recommendation to Congress that 30,500 acres be included in the wilderness system. According to the Santa Fe Group of the Sierra Club, this Forest Service recommendation is close to the number of acres that the group recommended be included. The deleted acreage in the Forest Service proposal includes the Goose Lake and Pioneer Lake sections where motorized trails already exist. The western boundary includes most of the high country above the villages of San Cristobal and Arroyo Hondo. To the north, the boundary lies close to NM 38; to the east, it runs along the ridge of Gold Hill; and to the south, it parallels NM 150 but excludes Bull-of-the Woods and West Fork trails. The Sierra Club believes, however, that the proposed Columbine-Hondo area should be united with the Wheeler Peak Wilderness Area to form one wilderness. The powerline that separates the two areas (along Bull-of-the-Woods and West Fork trails) would be a narrow corridor excluded from the wilderness.

YERBA CANYON TRAIL #61—MANZANITA CANYON TRAIL #58 LOOP

Length: 9 miles round trip
Degree of Difficulty: Difficult
Elevation: 8,400-11,600 feet
Maps: Latir Peak and Wheeler Peak Wilderness; USGS Arroyo Seco
Finding the Trailhead: Take NM 150, the Taos Ski Valley highway, 10.1 miles from the junction of NM 522 north of Taos. You can park alongside the highway at the Yerba Canyon trailhead, or if you have a high-clearance vehicle you can drive the short road left (north) off the highway that ends at the wilderness boundary. The sign here says it's 5 miles to Lobo Peak (the trail itself is 3.9 miles) and 12 miles to Gold Hill.

If combined for a loop, these two trails provide a rigorous hike up into the high country near Lobo Peak. The described route goes up Yerba Canyon Trail to Lobo Peak and descends Manzanita Canyon Trail back to NM 150. You'll have to walk along the highway for about a mile back to your car at the Yerba Canyon trailhead. For those hikers wanting a more leisurely hike, you can hike either trail as far as you like, then return back down the same trail.

The trail follows the creek through the narrow canyon with numerous crossings. You can usually find a log to climb across—look for the spur trails people have made to these crossings. The vegetation is lush, with geranium, squaw lettuce, and baneberry growing profusely. The first several miles of the trail are only moderately steep. As you reach the aspen-covered hillsides, the terrain becomes steeper and there are fewer creek crossings.

A series of switchbacks on the right (east) side of the creek takes you up above the water, and the terrain gets even steeper. After a mile, the trail levels out as it swings around to the left (west) and crosses the canyon to the west side of the creek (you are above the spring that feeds the creek). There's an obvious campsite in a clearing. The trail crosses another spring and starts climbing straight up the canyon. It can sometimes be difficult to follow, but there are cairns (rock piles) that mark the route and old forest service blazes on the trees.

The trail turns to the west, then back to the east up some more switchbacks before cresting at the ridge, just to the southwest of

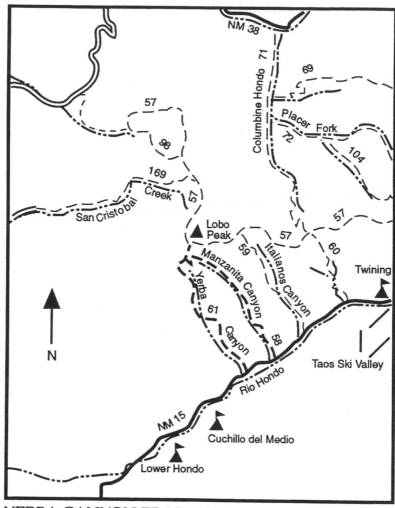

YERBA CANYON TRAIL #61; MANZANITA CANYON TRAIL #58

Lobo Peak. Turn right (east) and follow the trail up a little ways to the junction with Manzanita Canyon Trail, which turns right (south). If you wait to descend Manzanita Canyon and continue along the trail towards the peak, you'll come to some incredible views. To the north, you can see over towards San Cristobal

Canyon; to the east, beyond Lobo Peak, you can just see to Gold Hill. And to the south, the whole magnificent panorama of the Sangre de Cristos, from the slopes of Taos Ski Valley to Wheeler Peak, spreads before you. The trail you are on continues up to Lobo Peak, where it divides and goes east to Gold Hill and north to Flag Mountain (and connects with trails from San Cristobal and Lama).

Manzanita Canyon Trail (4.2 miles) heads down the west side of the canyon; watch for tree blazes to guide you. After a short distance, the trail switchbacks sharply to the left (north) and continues down the canyon to the stream, where it turns back to the south. It follows the east side of the canyon here, and affords periodic views of Wheeler Peak. The trail heads away from the stream and follows a ridge between the stream you crossed and another stream to the east. It eventually crosses this stream as well, in a steep descent, then picks up the main creek that flows all the way down the canyon. You'll pass through several aspen stands before the trail switchbacks down to the creekside, where again there are numerous crossings as you descend the canyon.

The terrain levels out near the creek, and after about a mile the trail widens to a road, which leads another mile to the highway. A sign at the trailhead says it's 5 miles to Lobo Peak. Another mile walk down NM 150 will bring you back to your car.

GAVILAN CANYON TRAIL #60—ITALIANOS CANYON TRAIL #59 LOOP

Length: 8¹/₂ miles round trip
Degree of Difficulty: Difficult
Elevation: 8,800-11,700 feet
Maps: Latir Peak and Wheeler Peak Wilderness; USGS Arroyo Seco, Wheeler Peak, Red River
Finding the Trailhead: Take NM 150, the Taos Ski Valley highway, 13.2 miles from the junction of NM 522 north of Taos to the Gavilan trailhead. There is room to park at the trailhead.

This is a good hike to take in late summer, as the tasty thimbleberry grows all along both trails. These two trails, like Yerba and Manzanita trails, lead up to the Lobo Peak area and can be hiked as a loop system. The hike begins at Gavilan Canyon Trail and returns along Italianos Canyon Trail. The Gavilan trail sign says it's 6 miles to Lobo Peak and 7 miles to Gold Hill (the trail itself is 2.4 miles).

Gavilan Canyon Trail travels through lush vegetation in a steep climb up the canyon. Besides thimbleberry you'll see geranium, wild parsley, and the unusual fern-like lousewort. The trail picks up the creek where it junctions with an old road. It crosses to the east side of the creek and switchbacks up the side of the canyon. The hike is quite steep for the next two miles as it climbs through mixed conifer vegetation.

In a large aspen meadow the trail levels out. Follow the creek up through the meadow (cairns also mark the route) and take a minute to look back over your shoulder at the view of Taos Ski Valley and Wheeler Peak. Bear to the left (west) at the head of the meadow (another route heads east up through the avalanche slide) into another meadow, where the trail steepens again. Climb straight up through the rock slide to another meadow where cairns will guide you left (west) into the trees. Steep switchbacks lead you to the top of the ridge and the junction with Trail #57, which heads right (east) to Gold Hill, and left (west) to Lobo Peak. The Columbine Trail also junctions here and continues north about 5 miles to Columbine Campground on the highway to Red River. The view extends in all directions—east to Gold Hill, south to Wheeler Peak, west to Lobo Peak, and north to the Molycorp mine scar near Red River.

Turn left (west) and follow Trail #57 as it climbs the steep ridge towards Lobo Peak. At the top of the ridge you can once again see views in all directions. The trail turns northwest, climbs down off the ridge, levels out, and circles the head of Italianos Canyon. At about 1½ miles the trail enters the trees and junctions with Italianos Canyon Trail #59. There is no view here.

Follow Italianos Canyon Trail in a steep descent to the southeast. Cairns mark the route on this upper portion of the trail through the meadows. Once into the first meadow, views of Wheeler Peak open up. The trail follows a stream on the west side, then passes through another meadow where it picks up another stream and again crosses to the west side. Several more meadows are crossed; then the trail enters the mixed-conifer forest and returns to the stream. It crosses to the east side in a steep descent

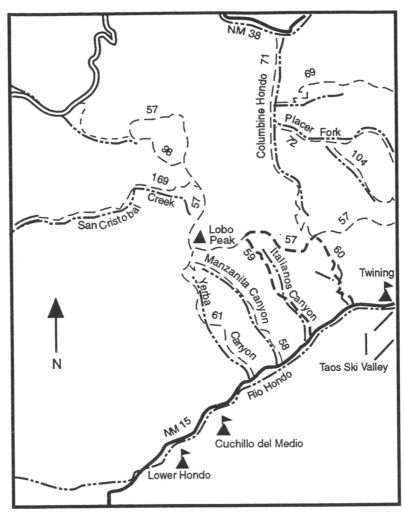

NM 38

Columbine Hondo 71

69

Placer Fork

72

104

57

98

169

Creek 57

San Cristobal

Lobo Peak

57

57

59

Italianos Canyon

60

Twining

Manzanita Canyon

Yerba

61

Canyon

58

Taos Ski Valley

N

Rio Hondo

NM 15

Cuchillo del Medio

Lower Hondo

GAVILAN TRAIL #60—ITALIANOS TRAIL #59 LOOP

down switchbacks; bluebells, larkspur, and cow parsnip grow profusely along the creek. Once the trail levels out there are numerous creek crossings, usually facilitated by strategically placed logs and rocks. At the trailhead walk 1 mile east back to your car at the Gavilan Canyon trailhead.

View to Wheeler Peak

BULL-OF-THE-WOODS TRAIL #90—LONG CANYON TRAIL #63—GOLD HILL TRAIL #64 LOOP

Length: 7 1/2 miles
Degree of Difficulty: Difficult
Elevation: 9,500-12,700 feet
Maps: Latir Peak and Wheeler Peak Wilderness; USGS Wheeler Peak, Red River
Finding the Trailhead: Take NM 150 to the Taos Ski Valley; Bull-of-the-Woods Trail begins at the northeast corner of the valley parking lot where the road turns south to the private home area and Williams Lake Trail. A Forest Serviced sign marks the trailhead on the east side of the parking lot.

You can use Bull-of-the-Woods Trail to access a loop hike that leads you north into the Columbine-Hondo area of Gold Hill above the Red River Valley. Bull-of-the-Woods heads straight uphill to the east on the north side of East Fork Rio Hondo and the south side of the power line. Maintain an easterly course as the trail crosses several power line openings until you reach the last

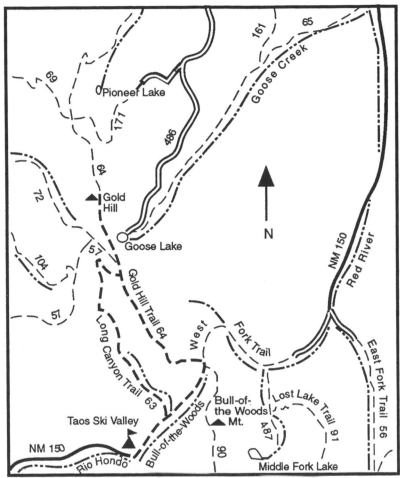

BULL-OF-THE-WOODS TRAIL #90—LONG CANYON TRAIL #63— GOLD HILL TRAIL #64

pole. Follow the arrow pointing left, up a short hill, where the trail turns northeast again as it follows the creek.

At about 1 mile the trail crosses a forest road; signs indicate the junction with Columbine-Twining National Recreation Trail to the left (northwest). Long Canyon Trail leads 4¹/₂ miles to Gold Hill and 13 miles to Columbine Campground. Bull-of-the-Woods continues to the right (east). Just beyond this junction, a road heads right (south) back to the Taos Ski Valley. The trail to Bull-of-the Woods becomes a road here as well; continue east to where the trail switchbacks to the south. Follow the switchback south, and at the top of the hill you can see down over the valley to the Taos llano. The road then turns back northeast in a direct ascent to Bull-of-the-Woods Pasture, a large grassy area, at the top of the ridge.

Gold Hill Trail #64 heads northwest 3 miles to Gold Hill and Goose Lake. West Fork River Trail, which leads 3 miles down to FR 58 on the Red River side of the mountains, heads north across the meadow. Gold Hill Trail climbs steadily into mixed-conifer forest to a view over your shoulder of Kachina Peak in Taos Ski Valley. After about a mile the terrain levels out as the trail reaches a meadow. Ahead, you can see the ridge that leads west to Lobo Peak and east to Gold Hill. Behind you can see the high peaks surrounding the ski valley. The trail continues uphill into the trees through a series of meadows; fuchsia-colored sky pilot and bright red rose crown color the terrain. An old mining cabin and tailings indicate the turn left (west) towards the sign in the meadow at the junction of Long Canyon Trail. For a view of Goose Lake and Gold Hill, continue up the ridge from the cabin. Goose Lake sits down below, to the northeast, where both a trail and four-wheel drive road lead down to the town of Red River. Gold Hill is straight ahead, the high point on the ridge.

To continue the loop climb back down to the sign in the meadow, where Long Canyon Trail heads west. Gold Hill Trail continues north, up the ridge, to the junction with Trail #72, which heads north to Columbine Campground, and Trail #57, which heads west to Lobo Peak. Follow the cairns through the meadow. Long Canyon Trail crosses the head of the canyon to the west, then turns sharply down into the drainage along the east side. It picks up the creek in a lovely meadow, a perfect campsite. The trail stays on the east side of the creek the entire 2 1/2 miles back to Bull-of-the-Woods Trail. Turn right (west) on Bull-of-the-Woods Trail back to the Taos Ski Valley.

Section VI. Wheeler Peak

The Wheeler Peak Wilderness is a small but spectacular wilderness that is home to New Mexico's highest peak—Wheeler. The 19,150-acre wilderness encompasses the culturally significant and spectacularly beautiful high-country ridge between the Taos Ski Valley to the west, or the old Twining gold mine, and the Red River Valley to the east. Much of the area is above timberline, and you will find plants and animals here not common to the rest of the hikes described in this book: The marmot and pika burrow in meadows and rock slides, while moss campion, alpine forget-me-nots, and stonecrop color the tundra expanse. The remnants of the extensive mining activity of the late nineteenth and early twentieth century litter the way to Bull-of-the-Woods Mountain and beyond. But these remains enhance rather than detract from the wilderness experience the area offers, providing a sense of the indomitable human spirit.

BULL-OF-THE-WOODS TRAIL #90—CREST RIDGE TRAIL #90 (to Wheeler Peak)

Length: 14 miles round trip
Degree of Difficulty: Difficult
Elevation: 9,500-13,161 feet
Maps: Latir Peak and Wheeler Peak Wilderness; USGS Wheeler Peak
Finding the Trailhead: Take NM 150 to the Taos Ski Valley; Bull-of-the-Woods Trail begins at the northeast corner of the valley parking lot where the road turns south to the private home area and Williams Lake Trail.

Twining Gold Camp

Back in the 19th century, before the concept of a downhill ski area even existed, the Taos Ski Valley was the home of two gold mining camps, Amizette, along the Rio Hondo just below the present day ski area, and Twining, where the ski area now sits. In the late 1890s William Fraser, Al Helphenstine, and two others struck significant veins of silver and gold along the Rio Hondo. The area was already accessible to miners because of a road Fraser had built, and soon a hotel and adjoining townsite became Amizette, named for Helphenstine's wife. Several large mining companies purchased claims in Amizette, and there was even talk of a railroad coming to the canyon, but by 1895 Amizette was already a ghost town, the ores having proved too spotty and low grade.

However, Fraser continued staking claims higher up in the canyon, where the Rio Hondo and Lake Fork converge. After much trial and error, and the discovery of significant amounts of copper ore (from which gold could be extracted), Fraser concentrated his efforts on Fraser Mountain. In 1901 Albert C. Twining and a group of New Jersey capitalists purchased controlling interest of Fraser's company and incorporated the Fraser Mountain Copper Company. Soon the support site at the end of Hondo Canyon, referred to as Twining, was the site of a lumber mill, smelter, hotel, smith shop, storehouse, and company housing and headquarters. Water powered an electric plant, and telephone lines connected the community and plant. The first trial run of the smelter was in June of 1903. Unfortunately, the molten ore and stone clung to the sides of the cauldron and had to be broken out with picks. When the second trial resulted in the same ore freeze, a $300,000 investment proved worthless. By the end of the summer, Fraser Mountain Copper Company went into the hands of a receiver, Twining was bankrupt, and the claims reverted to Fraser. He continued to try to convince investors to commit capital to his properties. After selling his property for $85,000 to a man named Jack Bidwell from New York, Fraser tried to back out of the deal, ended up in court, and then tried to reclaim his Fraser Mountain properties by force. On July 16, 1914, Fraser confronted Bidwell, who was in Twining to run the mine, and shot at him with a six-shooter. Bidwell ran into a bunkhouse, emerged from the back door with a .30-30 Winchester, and shot Fraser between the eyes when he turned around at the sound of his voice. Bidwell was acquitted and continued to live in Twining for a number of years, but by 1924 all the cabins and hotel had been razed, and in 1932 the smelter was destroyed by fire. Ernie Blake, founder of the Taos Ski Valley, arrived in the 1950s, and Twining ceased to exist.

The Hike

A day hike to Wheeler Peak is not as hard as the 14-mile length might indicate, as the Crest Ridge Trail is well defined and crosses little or no talus (loose rock). For those who don't want to attempt the ascent, a 4-mile round-trip hike can be made up Bull-of-the-Woods Trail to Bull-of-the-Woods Pasture, where a small pond provides a good lunch spot. If you do decide to climb Wheeler Peak, get an early start and try to pick a time of the year when afternoon thunderstorms will not prevent you from making it to the peak.

Bull-of-the-Woods heads straight uphill to the east on the north side of East Fork Rio Hondo and the south side of the power line. Maintain an easterly course as the trail crosses several power line openings until you reach the last pole. Follow the arrow pointing left, up a short hill, where the trail turns northeast again as it follows the creek.

At about 1 mile the trail crosses a forest road; signs indicate the junction with Columbine-Twining National Recreation Trail to the left (northwest). Long Canyon Trail leads 4$^{1}/_{2}$ miles to Gold Hill and 13 miles to Columbine Campground. Bull-of-the-Woods continues to the right (east). Just beyond this junction, a road heads right (south) back to the Taos Ski Valley. The trail to Bull-of-the-Woods becomes a road here as well; continue east to where the trail switchbacks to the south. Follow the switchback south, and at the top of the hill you can see down over the valley to the Taos llano. The road then turns back northeast in a direct ascent to Bull-of-the-Woods Pasture, a large grassy area, at the top of the ridge.

Gold Hill Trail #64 heads northwest 3 miles to Gold Hill and Goose Lake. West Fork River Trail, which leads 3 miles down to FR 58 on the Red River side of the mountains, heads north across the meadow.

A sign indicates Crest Ridge Trail #90, which climbs the road up to the ridge, where you have a view of both the Taos Ski Valley to the west and the Red River Valley to the east. Arrows guide you

At the top of Wheeler Peak

along the road as it turns southeast. The road climbs steeply to a junction at the ridgeline above Red River; the road continues left (north) to an old mine site; to the right, it narrows to a trail at the fenceline. The sign says Old Mike Peak Trail, the former name of Crest Ridge Trail.

Switchbacks leads up into the trees for a short distance, then the trail heads out into open terrain. It traverses the east side with views of the Red River Valley, then crosses over to the west side as it climbs around Bull-of-the-Woods Mountain. You can see the old mining road below the trail and Lake Fork Peak above the ski valley. Once around the mountain, the trail crosses back to the east side, where the lake you see down below is Middle Fork Lake, accessed from NM 150 in Red River. Alpine wildflowers grow profusely all along the trail—moss campion, alpine-forget-me-nots, and columbines.

The trail descends into the headwaters of the Middle Fork Red River, the only water available on the hike. Back in this mixed-conifer environment you'll see the beautiful parry primrose and marsh marigold. The trail quickly climbs back out of this drainage into what is called La Cal Basin, a bowl between ridges on both

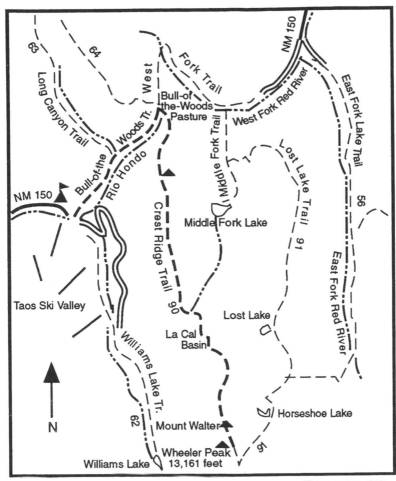

BULL-OF-THE-WOODS TRAIL #90—CREST RIDGE TRAIL #90

east and west sides. Here you'll start to see the ubiquitous high-country marmot, fat and sleek creatures who are obviously acclimated to human presence—watch out for your food if you stop to eat.

The trail climbs in long switchbacks out of the basin to a saddle below Mount Walter. Here, to the east, you can see Horseshoe

Lake, accessed from the East Fork Red River or Lost Lake Trail. Various routes lead from the lake up to Wheeler. It's not that steep a climb up to the top of Walter, where a marker indicates the elevation (13,141 feet). From Walter you can see over to Wheeler Peak, less than 1/2 mile farther along the trail. The trail climbs down from Walter, then up towards Wheeler; a spur trail to the right climbs the last few feet to the marker, giving the elevation, 13,161 feet, and a short explanation that the peak was named for Major George M. Wheeler, who surveyed this area as well as many other peaks in the southwestern states. A stone wall provides shelter from the prevailing winds, where you might want to sit while you sign the book encased in a metal pipe in the marker. The last time I was on Wheeler we read through some of the book and found this interesting entry: "5 man party, 2 men lost, 1 man lost toe to frost, no food, no water, no O2, God Have Mercy on our Souls"! The view is, of course, panoramic and inspiring (as indicated by many of the other entries). Make sure you keep an eye on the weather and leave the mountain before any dangerous clouds roll in. Crest Ridge Trail continues south to Simpson Peak.

WILLIAMS LAKE TRAIL #62

Length: 4 1/2 miles
Degree of Difficulty: Moderate
Elevation: 9,400-11,000 feet
Maps: Latir Peak and Wheeler Peak Wilderness; USGS Wheeler Peak
Finding the Trailhead: Take NM 150 to the Taos Ski Valley; follow the road south through the condominium and cabin area. The third switchback leads north through private land to Bull-of-the-Woods Trail; stay on the main road until you come to a parking pull-off for wilderness access near the new restaurant below Kachina Chairlift. Walk along the road to the Phoenix Restaurant and chairlift, where Williams Lake Trail turns south.

The Naming of Mountains

Many of the highest mountains in our western states are named for the geologists and surveyors who were involved in

Climbing Wheeler Peak from Williams Lake

their exploration. Major George M. Wheeler of the United States Army was involved in the mapping of of New Mexico between the years of 1871 and 1878. The highest mountain in New Mexico, Wheeler Peak, 13, 161 feet in elevation, now bears his name, as do several other peaks in Nevada and California. It was not until 1948, however, that Wheeler Peak was acknowledged as the state's highest peak. Until that time it was thought that the Truchas Peaks, to the southeast of Wheeler, were higher. Harold M. Walter, a resident of Santa Fe and avid mountaineer and photographer, is credited with verifying that Wheeler was indeed the highest mountain. According to Bob Julyan in *The Place Names of New Mexico*, "Knowing that the knob north of Wheeler was unnamed, Walter began calling it Mount Walter, for himself, but the name could not become official until after his death in 1958. A plaque on the mountain commemorates Walter, 'who loved these mountains.' " Fraser (or Frazer, as it appears on Forest Service maps) Mountain, to the north of Mount Walter and Wheeler Peak, is named for William Fraser, who along with Al Helphenstine, discovered the gold strikes that led to the founding of the Amizette and Twining mining camps in Hondo Canyon (see page 54). He also founded the Fraser Mountain Copper Mines, farther east, thus naming the peak. He died ignominiously with a bullet hole through his head in a dispute with a former partner.

The Hike

This is the route that most hikers take on their way to Wheeler Peak. Williams Lake sits in a glacial cirque 4$1/2$ miles from the Taos Ski Valley. The high wilderness peaks loom ahead—Kachina Peak is off to the right. At the chairlift, continue south along the Rio Hondo a short distance to where the road forks; bear left (southeast) along the stream, as the road to the rights turns and circles back to the chairlift. About $1/2$ mile up the road narrows to a trail, and a marker indicates that Williams Lake is 2 miles farther.

The trail leaves the stream and continues its southeast climb through the trees to a meadow. Behind you appear the high peaks of the Gold Hill area. The trail passes through boulder fields and east-side talus slopes to the Wheeler Peak Wilderness boundary sign, about 1 mile from the chairlift. From here it's a steady climb through the trees to the saddle above Williams Lake. Camping is restricted around the lake to preserve the shoreline.

From the lake it's 1.4 miles up a primitive trail to Wheeler Peak. The trail to the Peak begins on the east side of the lake,

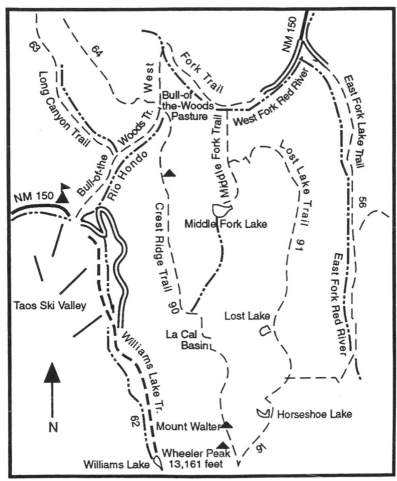

Map labels: NM 150, Fork Trail, Bull-of-the-Woods Pasture, West Fork Red River, East Fork Lake Trail, Long Canyon Trail, West Woods Tr., Bull-of-the Woods Tr., Rio Hondo, Middle Fork Trail, Lost Lake Trail, 91, 56, NM 150, Crest Ridge Trail, Middle Fork Lake, East Fork Red River, Taos Ski Valley, 90, Lost Lake, Williams Lake Tr., La Cal Basin, N, 62, Mount Walter, Horseshoe Lake, Williams Lake, Wheeler Peak 13,161 feet, 6, 64, 63

WILLIAMS LAKE TRAIL #62

through a narrow canyon to the slopes of the peak. While there is a visible trail the entire climb, much of it is covered with slippery talus, and the elevatin gain is extreme. It takes most hikers more than an hour to complete the climb to the top of Wheeler.

Section VII. Red River

The trails accessed from the town of Red River lie on the east side of the Sangre de Cristos just over the ridge from the previously described Columbine-Hondo and Wheeler Peak trails. Consequently, many of these trails connect with each other, and routes can be hiked that lead from the Taos Ski Valley to Red River. Other hikes in the area lie near the Red River Ski Area and can be accessed from the downhill slopes and old logging and mining roads that lead west from the town.

COLUMBINE-TWINING RECREATION TRAIL #71
Length: 10 miles round trip to Cow Lake Junction
Degree of Difficulty: Easy to Moderate
Elevation: 8,000-11,200 feet
Maps: Latir Peak and Wheeler Peak Wilderness; USGS Red River
Finding the Trailhead: Take NM 38 east from Questa 5.2 miles to Columbine Canyon Campground. Turn right into the campground and follow the one-way road around to the south-side trailhead. A sign here says it's 9 miles to Gold Hill, 10 miles to Lobo Peak, and 13 miles to Twining (the Taos Ski Valley).

This is the main artery into the proposed Columbine-Hondo Wilderness from the north side. It connects with several interior trails that lead to Gold Hill, and at its termination connects to the trails which access the proposed wilderness from NM 150 in the Taos Ski Valley. A good day hike along Trail #71 leads to the junction of Cow Lake Trail #96 (a non-maintained trail) in a beautiful meadow below Lobo Peak. Trail #71 continues another steep mile to its terminus on top of the Lobo Peak ridge. The entire length of the trail is 5.7 miles.

The hike up the first several miles of the trail alongside Columbine Creek is quite easy. There are numerous creek cross-

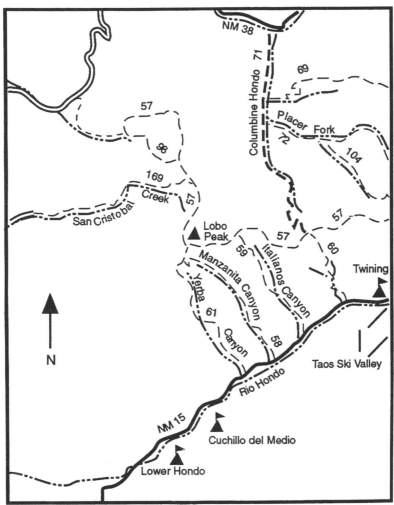

COLUMBINE-TWINING RECREATION TRAIL #71

ings, but bridges and strategically placed logs provide access. This is one of the most beautiful canyons in the Carson: larkspur, harebell, monarda (wild oregano), thimbleberry, and raspberry line the trail surrounded by steep canyon walls. It's a little less than 2 miles to the junction with Trail #69, which climbs along Deer

Creek in a steep ascent to Gold Hill. Columbine Trail continues another 1/2 mile to the next junction with Trail #72, which also leads to Gold Hill. Just past this junction, where the trail crosses the creek to the west side, a spur trail has been blazed that stays on the east side of the creek. Both trails meet at the next creek crossing.

The trail soon steepens as it continues to follow the creek. A switchback takes you up the east side high above the water but the trail quickly returns to the lush riparian corridor, where cow parsnip and monkshood thrive next to small waterfalls. Watch for the cairns (rock trail markers) that guide you across the creek to the west. Again follow cairns across the next meadow and drainage. The trail leaves the creek and momentarily levels as it continues through another meadow where you can see ahead to the Lobo Peak ridge. The trail then enters a large, beautiful meadow where a trail sign indicates the junction with Cow Lake Trail #96, which leads southwest to Cow Lake but is not maintained for public use. The meadow provides a lovely lunch spot (or good campsite if you're backpacking) for those hikers who want to stop here. Columbine Trail #71 continues for another mile in a steep ascent to the Lobo Peak ridge, where it intersects Trail #57, which leads east to Gold Hill and west to Lobo Peak, and Gavilan Trail #60, which leads south to NM 150. If you choose to continue up the ridge, watch for cairns that mark the route through the meadow south and the switchback to the east up the reconstructed trail (water bars across the trail mark the route). Just below the ridge a large boulder field provides your first view north across Columbine Canyon to Flag Mountain. The view on top of the ridge is panoramic.

GOOSE LAKE TRAIL #65

Length: 12 miles round trip
Degree of Difficulty: Difficult
Elevation: 9,200-11,000 feet
Maps: Latir Peak and Wheeler Peak Wilderness; USGS Red River
Finding the Trailhead: The trailhead is located 2.1 miles from the junction of NM 38 and NM 150 on NM 150 (new numbering by the highway department now signs NM 150 as NM 578, but on all the forest maps it's still listed as NM 150). You'll pass the four

Remnants of mine above Goose Lake

wheel drive road junction, which also says Goose Lake Trail, at .6 miles. There's room to park your car at a pull-off near the Aspen Ranch sign.

Red River Mining

All over the Red River Valley are the names that reveal its long history of gold rush fever—Placer Creek, Gold Hill, Caribel, Pioneer Creek, Mallette Creek. Named for the men who came and the activity they pursued, these places are today the home of a resort industry that is a direct descendant of a century of mining.

Before the town of Red River existed, miners had established the short-lived communities of La Belle, to the northeast, and Elizabethtown, to the southeast. Elizabethtown, first settled in the mid-19th century, was the site of an engineering feat as well: Under the direction of the infamous Lucien Maxwell, a 40-mile system of flumes and canals—the "Big Ditch"—carried water from the upper Red River through the mountains to the Elizabethtown mines in the Moreno Valley. Remnants of the "Big Ditch" are still visible along the trails in upper Red River Valley.

After various busts and booms, the town of Red River became the center of the mining activity in the late 19th century, eclipsing both Elizabethtown and LaBelle despite being inaccessible from either Questa or over the steep mountain pass from Elizabethtown. While the "big" strike never came, and the cost of shipping low-grade ore out of the valley for processing was prohibitive, the town survived. In 1916 the Forest Service built a new road over the pass south into Colfax County, and while one by one the mines closed in the 1920s, a new industry kept the town alive— tourism. Lured by the valley's beauty and the town father's boosterism, Red River became a resort town. By the end of World War II, the town was considered one of the premier vacation spots in the Rocky Mountains. When the Red River Ski Area became a reality in the 1950s, the area became a year-round resort. Only the names remain to remind you of the miners who scrambled all over the mountains and valleys to secure their claims and maybe make it rich.

The Hike

Most of the trails out of the town of Red River are open to ATV use, but Goose Lake Trail is primarily a hiking trail, as a four-wheel drive road also accesses the lake along a different route. Bear left across the bridge, and Goose Lake Trail follows Goose Creek up into thick spruce-fir vegetation in a moderate climb. A sign says it's 6 miles to Goose Lake and 7 miles to Gold Hill. The trail crosses over to the south side of the creek and passes through a gate. It then crosses back to the north side and passes through another gate. The hills next to the trail at this lower elevation are covered with both scarlet penstemon and skyrocket gilia, which look very much alike until you look closely at the star-shaped flower head of the gilia. The trail crosses several small meadows (I saw a deer leap across one of the meadows the last time I was there).

Once past the meadows, the terrain becomes somewhat steeper. Where the trail forks, stay to the right (the trail to the left just goes to the river). At about 2½ miles, you'll reach the junction with Trail #161, which leads to the four-wheel drive road that also

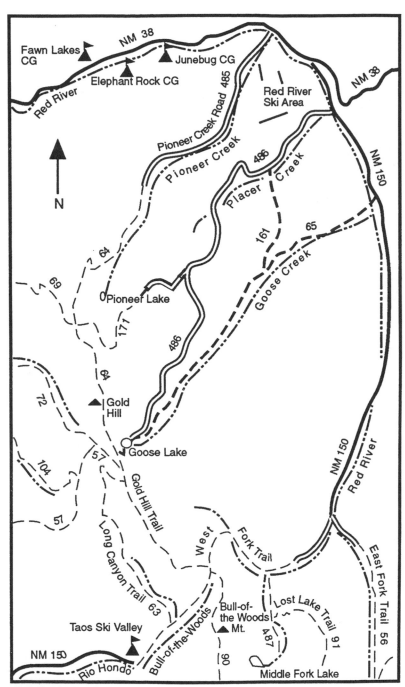

GOOSE LAKE TRAIL #65

accesses Goose Lake. Continue straight ahead on Trail #65.

The trail passes through an obvious campsite and immediately crosses the creek to the south side. After climbing for awhile it crosses back to the north side, where you might see the lovely shooting star. The terrain is more level here until the trail crosses to the south side and climbs again to the boggy area just below the lake. At a swampy meadow the trail circles to the right and stays to the right until you reach a short, steep climb up to the lake, nestled below Gold Hill. A sign just before you reach the lake says the trail back down to the highway is 4³/4 miles, but I think it's closer to the 6 miles the first sign indicated. It's 1 mile up to Gold Hill Trail (you can see the trail switchbacking up the ridge just to the south of Gold Hill), and 8 miles down the four-wheel drive road to the highway. The road terminates farther north on the lake, so you can rest in relative peace before beginning your descent.

WEST FORK TRAIL #175

Length: 8 miles round trip
Degree of Difficulty: Moderate
Elevation: 9,500-10,800 feet
Maps: Latir Peak and Wheeler Peak Wilderness; USGS Wheeler Peak
Finding the Trailhead: Follow NM 150 6 miles south out of Red River to the end of the pavement, then west along FR 58 to the parking area for Middle Fork and West Fork trails. Leave your car here.

This trail is accessed off NM 150, where many of the trails leading into the Wheeler Peak Wilderness begin. It leads up to Bull-of-the-Woods Pasture and to the trails in the Columbine-Hondo area. A few hundred yards farther along the four-wheel drive road is the turnoff to Middle Fork Lake and Lost Lake trails. Cross under the gate and continue along the road to access West Fork Trail. The road is a gradual ascent as it follows the powerline through this pocket of private land along the river. The road periodically leaves the powerline as it follows the West Fork through a meadow area, then past a boarded-up cabin. At about ³/4 mile, the power line turns sharply west to ascend the ridge towards Bull-of-

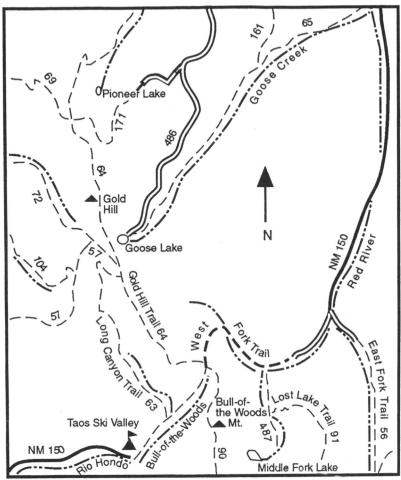

WEST FORK TRAIL #175

the-Woods, and the road winds around to the right (northwest). Raspberries grow all along the path and are usually ripe by late August. Views of the valley open up behind you.

The road steepens as it begins to narrow to a trail, and a broken sign at the foot of a post indicates that the trail bears left, towards the river, while the road circles around to the right. Follow the trail across the slope to the river crossing and continue up into the trees. A short distance uphill another signless post stands at what looks like a trail junction; bear right, up through the trees. There is considerable downfall here, and you have to look carefully to find the trail as it switchbacks up the hill.

After about a half mile the trail reaches the power easement (old poles are still standing) and heads up the easement towards Bull-of-the-Woods. It's a short but steep climb to Bull-of-the-Woods Meadow, a large pasture full of yarrow and fringed gentians. The trail skirts the meadow to the west, past a horse corral, to a campsite near a small pond and the junction with the trails heading to Wheeler Peak, Gold Hill, and the Taos Ski Valley. Gold Hill Trail #64 heads northwest 3 miles to Gold Hill and Goose Lake; Bull-of-the-Woods Trail heads 2 miles west down to the Taos Ski Valley; and Crest Ridge Trail #90 heads south 5 miles to Wheeler Peak. Climb a little ways up Trail #90 for a view of both the Taos Ski Valley to the west and the Red River Valley to the east.

Section VIII. Tres Ritos

The trails in this section are accessed from NM 518 southeast from Ranchos de Taos to Mora. Most of them are east of NM 75, the highway to Peñasco, in a heavily used recreation area used by both local people and visitors from Texas. I've indicated which of these trails are open to ATV use and which are restricted to hiking and horseback use. To avoid meeting off-road vehicles on the trails, it's best to hike these trails during the off-season, early summer and fall.

AMOLE CANYON TRAIL #10
Length: 4 miles round trip
Degree of Difficulty: Easy
Elevation: 8,200-9,200 feet
Maps: Trails Illustrated Carson National Forest; USGS Tres Ritos
Finding the Trailhead: From Taos drive 14.6 miles south on NM 518 (from the junction with NM 68) to Forest Road 703, on the east side of the highway. If you're coming from the Peñasco area, FR 703 is 1.6 miles on NM 518 from the junction with NM 75. You can leave your car at the pull-off alongside the highway or drive directly to the trailhead on FR 703.

Follow the forest road into the Amole Canyon cross-country ski area. At about one quarter mile you'll see the turn left onto the first cross-country ski loop. Continue along the road and as it begins to curve south another sign indicates the upper and lower ski loops to the left (north). This is the start of Amole Canyon Trail #10 (the last time I was there the trail sign numbered the trail #4). This is an old logging road and is birmed to prevent vehicular access.

FT #10 climbs through ponderosa pine into spruce-fir vegetation and soon passes the junction with one of the returning ski

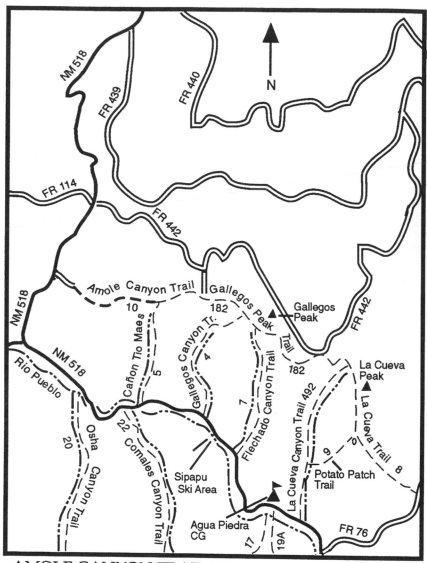

AMOLE CANYON TRAIL #10

trails. At about 1³/₄ miles up the trail an arrow indicates that the ski trails turn sharply to the left. Continue ahead, along the road, and in about $^1/_4$ mile you'll reach the junction with Cañon Tio Maes. Beyond this junction, Amole Canyon Trail becomes Gallegos Peak Trail #182, which continues east to Gallegos Peak. This part of the trail is described in the Cañon Tio Maes section.

OSHA CANYON TRAIL #20
Length: 14 miles round trip
Degree of Difficulty: Moderate
Elevation: 7,800-10,500 feet
Maps: Trails Illustrated Carson National Forest; USGS Tres Ritos
Finding the Trailhead: From the junction of NM 518 and NM 75 (to Peñasco) travel southeast 1.4 miles on 518 to the parking area at the Osha Canyon trail sign and park by the river. A signpost stands next to the trail; cross the Rio Pueblo over a conveniently placed log and follow the trail (an arrow indicates the way) up a short, steep climb above the Rio Pueblo into Osha Canyon.

This hike leads up Osha Canyon to the junction with Comales Canyon Trail, which in turn leads to Ripley's Point and the junction with Agua Piedra Trail and Indian Creek Trail. The trail levels out and stays on the north side of the canyon for the first half mile. After the trail reaches the Osha Canyon creek, numerous crossings can then make this a wet hike (the creek is actually quite narrow). It's a long 7 miles to the junction with Comales Trail, but day hikers can go as far as they like, then return down the same trail.

COMALES CANYON TRAIL #22—CORDOVA CANYON TRAIL #17
Length: 8 miles round trip
Degree of Difficulty: Moderate to Difficult
Elevation: 8,000-10,400 feet
Maps: Trails Illustrated Carson National Forest; USGS Tres Ritos
Finding the Trailhead: If you hike these trails as a loop, you need to leave a car at the Cordova Canyon trailhead and return to the Comales Canyon trailhead to begin the hike. Comales Canyon Trail is found 2.2 miles southeast on NM 518 from the junction of 518 and NM 75, the road to Peñasco (there is room to park up at

the top of the dirt road leading to the trailhead); Cordova Canyon trailhead is found in Agua Piedra Campground, 7 miles southeast of the junction of NM 518 and NM 75. Turn into the campground and follow the road through the gate to the right. Park at the birm.

It's best to begin this loop-hike on Comales Canyon Trail, as the upper reaches of the trail are obscured, and it is easier to follow it up than down. For those who want a more leisurely hike, follow the trail along the canyon bottom before it ascends to the junction with Cordova Canyon Trail and return the same way.

Comales Canyon Trail is a wet hike, as the trail follows the creek through this lower part of the trail, so wait until the waters have subsided in mid-summer. Sheer rock walls line the narrow canyon as you cross the creek numerous times and sometimes walk right through the creek bed. A steep climb brings you to a gate, above which are more creek crossings as the trail continues to climb. It levels out through a meadow as it follows the creek on the west side.

As the trail crosses to the east side, it passes through aspen groves, where the lovely monkshood grows. The trail then crosses the creek again and stays on the ridge between this main drainage and a subsidiary drainage to the west. There are a series of meadows along this upper portion of the trail as it heads towards Peñascoso Mountain, visible to the west. The trail then starts to curve around to the east, across the head of Comales Canyon, and can sometimes to difficult to follow as it passes through open terrain. Look for cairns that mark the way. The first time I hiked this loop I went up Cordova Canyon Trail and had a very difficult time finding Comales Canyon Tail through the upper meadows. I actually ended up following the western drainage until it connected with the trail in the lower part of the canyon.

You'll pass through a last stand of trees before the trail emerges into the meadow below the Cordova Canyon Trail junction. Several cairns mark the route up the meadow to the fenceline at the top of the ridge. Here the view is magnificent: Peñascoso Mountain defines the horizon to the west; to the north you can see Picuris Peak and on to Taos; to the east appears the Gallegos Peak area; and to the south you can see towards Ripley's Point. There is a gate in the fence and a large cairn marking the Cordova Canyon Trail junction. Comales Canyon Trail continues south to the junc-

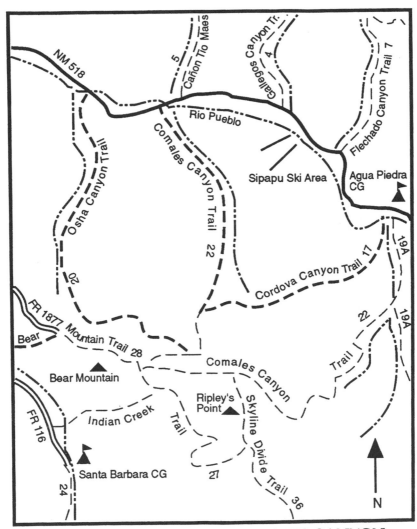

OSHA CANYON TRAIL #20; COMALES CANYON
TRAIL #22—CORDOVA CANYON TRAIL#17

tion with Osha Canyon Trail and on to Skyline Divide Trail.

Cordova Canyon Trail steeply descends to a "Y" in the trail, where a spur trail (the entire trail is actually a narrow four-wheel

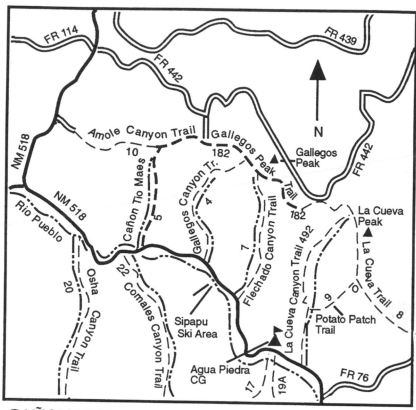

CAÑON TIO MAES TRAIL #5

drive road) ascends southwest towards Cordova Canyon (another place I momentarily lost the trail on my way up). Continue straight down the trail (you are heading east) into the head of Comales Canyon, where you'll cross the headwaters of Comales Creek.

The trail continues down through the trees to a meadow full of harebells and sebadillosos where it crosses a drainage and continues down across the meadow and back into the trees. The trail then swings to the left (north) for about a quarter mile before reaching another meadow. Bear to the right through the meadow to pick up the trail on the other side. A gradual descent leads through aspen groves as the trail travels closer to the canyon. A steep descent brings you to a gate where the trail continues along the wider road to the right to the main campground road, where a sign marks the trail.

CAÑON TIO MAES TRAIL #5

Length: 4 miles round trip
Degree of Difficulty: Easy
Elevation: 8,000-9,200 feet
Maps: Trails Illustrated Carson National Forest; USGS Tres Ritos
Finding the Trailhead: From the junction of NM 518 and NM 75 (to Peñasco) follow 518 southeast for 3.1 miles to the dirt road on the north side of the highway marking FT Cañon Tio Maes. Turn onto the road, then turn right onto the short road that leads to the trailhead. A sign indicates that FT 5 is open to motorcycles but closed to four-wheel drive vehicles.

This is a short, 2-mile hike up Cañon Tio Maes, but it can be made into a longer, 4-mile hike to Gallegos Peak in conjunction with Gallegos Peak Trail #182. I will describe both routes, and hikers can go as far as they choose. The trail heads north up the canyon following a creek the entire route. The first quarter mile is rather steep, but the trail then levels out into a moderate climb through mixed-conifer vegetation. After about a mile you'll reach a lovely aspen grove in a meadow; the trail then follows an easy route through more aspen stands to a clearing where it becomes more road-like. Several roads from the left (west) merge with FT 5 where it turns right (east) a short distance through the trees to a sign on a wide road indicating the turn west to Amole Canyon, FT 10. You can end your hike here, at about 2 miles in length, and return to your car the same way you came, or continue east to Gallegos Peak.

If you decide to continue the 2 more miles to Gallegos Peak, you can follow the continuation of Tio Maes Trail straight ahead, through the trees, along a quarter-mile hike to where the trail junctions with the same road you just crossed (on the map this road is numbered 182 to the east, 10 to the west). Or you can take a steep short-cut and turn east at the Amole Canyon sign, along

78

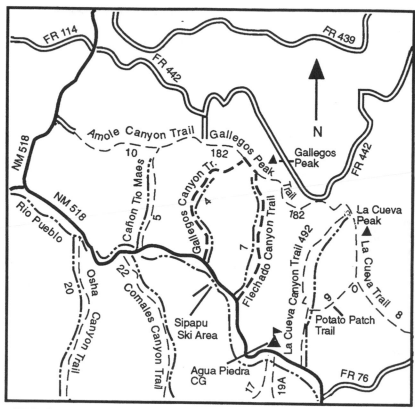

FLECHADO CANYON TRAIL #7—GALLEGOS CANYON TRAIL #4 LOOP

the road, and follow it to where the trail emerges from the trees (there's a trail sign here). You'll pass a corralled spring off to the right.

From here, the road levels out and continues east—you can see Gallegos Peak looming ahead. There are many old logging roads heading off in all directions, so be sure to stay on this main road. A short distance later a fenceline indicates the junction with an old logging road heading south from FR 442. Turn right onto the road, which the map shows is still FT 182. Continue along the road in a northeasterly direction. At a little over a mile you'll pass the Galle-

View from Gallegos Peak

gos and Flechado Canyon trailheads on the right, where the two trails head down to NM 518. A short distance farther on the road divides; follow the route to the right where it narrows to a trail. At a sign-less post it turns left, uphill, and climbs to the south side of Gallegos Peak. This south side of the peak is a wide, grassy meadow ringed by aspens. The view extends south to the Jicarita Peak ridge and on to Jicarilla Peak (Diamonte) and the Truchas Peaks. The trail continues along the south side of the peak and ties in with FR 442 on the northwest side. On the return trip remember to turn left at the fence or you'll end up on FR 442.

FLECHADO CANYON TRAIL #7—GALLEGOS CANYON TRAIL #4 LOOP

Length: 7 miles round trip
Degree of Difficulty: Easy to Moderate
Elevation: 8,200-10,000 feet
Maps: Trails Illustrated Carson National Forest; USGS Tres Ritos
Finding the Trailhead: From the junction of NM 518 and NM 75 (to Peñasco) follow 518 southeast for 5.4 miles to a pull-off where

View to Jicarita Ridge from Agua Piedra Trail

a sign indicates Flechado trailhead, or you can park at the campground just a few feet farther down the highway.

This is an easy 6-mile loop along two trails that lead north from NM 518 to Gallegos Peak. To make a complete loop you can leave your car at the Flechado trailhead, return along Gallegos Trail, and walk 1 mile south along the highway back to your car. Flechado Trail is closed to motor vehicles, but Gallegos Trail is not.

The trail climbs north from the highway along the west side of Flechado Canyon through lush vegetation. The first mile is fairly steep and rocky, alongside a creek. The trail reaches a meadow and levels out as it passes through aspen stands. There are several creek crossings before the trail steepens again and climbs through spruce-fir forest the last quarter mile to the junction with Gallegos Peak Trail #182 (an old four-wheel drive road), which leads west to FT 10 and Amole Canyon. To the east, just a short distance up the road, is Gallegos Peak. If you decide to climb to the peak, follow the road east to where it divides; turn right and the road narrows to a trail. At the sign-less post, turn left and follow the steep trail up to the south side of Gallegos Peak, where views extend south to the Jicarita Peak ridge and on to the Truchas Peaks.

Gallegos Canyon Trail is just to the west of the Flechado trailhead and is marked with a trail sign. It descends steeply down a wide path to a sign picturing a horse and rider, indicating a turn left. The trail follows the east side of the canyon down to an old road which parallels this horse route on the right.

The trail enters a rocky area between two meadows, and it's hard to believe that off-road vehicles travel this route. The trail momentarily divides, then becomes less rocky and steep and begins to resemble Flechado Trail as it becomes wet and lush. Some of the largest figwort plants I've ever seen fill a meadow shortly before the trail ends at NM 518. It's only a mile down the road to the left (south) back to your car, past the Sipapu Ski Area.

AGUA PIEDRA TRAIL #19A (to the Knob)

Length: 6 miles round trip
Degree of Difficulty: Easy to Moderate
Elevation: 8,400-10,000 feet
Maps: Trails Illustrated Carson National Forest; USGS Tres Ritos, Jicarita Peak
Finding the Trailhead: From the junction of NM 518 and NM 75 (to Peñasco) follow 518 southeast for 7 miles to Agua Piedra Campground. Turn into the campground and turn left just past the gate. Follow this road until it terminates at the horse corral. The trailhead lies to the south, at the top of the meadow.

ATVs and Hikers

There is always a certain amount of controversy generated when trails are open to both hikers and ATV (All Terrain Vehicle) use. On this east end of NM 518, ATVs have long been used by both locals and out-of-state visitors. However, because of budget constraints in the Forest Service and the fact that many of the trails, like Agua Piedra, are alongside creeks and rivers, there is concern that many of these trails cannot tolerate continued ATV use. Erosion of soils and contamination from vehicle emissions are the primary causes of concern. The Forest Service recently closed several trails to ATV use in the La Cueva Canyon area and has

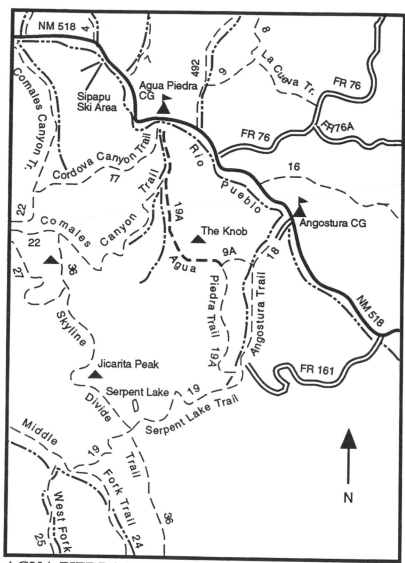

AGUA PIEDRA TRAIL #19A to the Knob

stated that unless it can come up with the money to reroute the trails on the south side of the highway, in the Agua Piedra area, the agency may consider closing them to ATVs. A local citizen group, the Rio Pueblo/Rio Embudo Watershed Protection Coalition, has recommended to the Forest Service that these south-side trails be open to hiking only, and that ATV use be concentrated in the La Junta Canyon area, on the north side of the highway. The group also plans to work with the Forest Service to install new metal signs that designate use on trails where signs have been stolen or vandalized.

The Hike

From Agua Piedra Campground you can follow Agua Piedra Trail to an area called the Knob, then return along the same route to the campground. The remainder of Agua Piedra Trail to Serpent Lake Trail is described in the Agua Piedra—Angostura Trail Loop section. On the Trails Illustrated map the first part of Agua Piedra Trail, from the campground to the junction with Comales Trail, is labeled Comales Trail. To avoid confusion, however, as most people refer to it as Agua Piedra Trail, I will call it that in these trail descriptions.

The trail follows the east side of Agua Piedra Creek for the first half mile in a gentle ascent. You must then cross the creek, which might mean getting your feet wet, as there is no easy way across. The trail continues south as it meanders through the creek area, crossing twice more before reaching the junction with Comales Trail #22. The sign here says it's 2 miles the way you came from Agua Piedra Campground, but unless you parked at the shelter by the highway, it's more like 1 mile from the trailhead. Comales Trail #22 (called Ripley's Point Trail on the sign) turns right (southwest) here and climbs to Ripley's Point and the junction with Skyline Divide Trail #36, which leads to Jicarita Peak (the trail to Ripley's Point is described in the next section).

Our route along Agua Piedra Trail #19A (the sign refers to it as Serpent Lake Trail) continues south, along the west side of the creek, in a steady climb. After about a mile the terrain steepens and the trail follows a more circuitous route through the trees for a quarter mile to a fence and clearing. The mountain to your left is called the Knob; a spur trail leads to the top near the fenceline and connects with an unmaintained trail that descends into the Rio Pueblo canyon.

The trail continues southeast through several clearings before descending to the meadow that marks the junction with Trail 9A, which leads east to Angostura Campground. In this meadow you can see the Jicarita Peak Ridge to the west, where pockets of snow are visible all summer long. This is a good place for lunch before returning along the same route back to Agua Piedra Campground. Agua Piedra Trail continues south to Serpent Lake Trail and FR 161, and is described in the Agua Piedra—Angostura Trail Loop section.

AGUA PIEDRA TRAIL #19A—COMALES CANYON TRAIL #22 (to Ripley's Point)

Length: 8 miles round trip
Degree of Difficulty: Moderate to Difficult
Elevation: 8,400-11,800 feet
Maps: Trails Illustrated Carson National Forest; USGS Tres Ritos, Jicarita Peak
Finding the Trailhead: From the junction of NM 518 and NM 75 (to Peñasco) follow 518 southeast for 7 miles to Agua Piedra Campground. Turn into the campground and turn left just past the gate. Follow this road until it terminates at the horse corral. The trailhead lies to the south, at the top of the meadow.

This hike begins at Agua Piedra Campground and follows Agua Piedra Trail to the junction with Comales Trail, which leads to Ripley's Point on Jicarita Peak ridge.

The first half mile of the trail follows the east side of Agua Piedra Creek, then crosses over to the west side and meanders through the creek area to the junction with Comales Trail #22. The sign at the junction calls this trail Ripley's Point Trail, and refers to Agua Piedra Trail #19 as Serpent Lake Trail. Agua Piedra Trail continues south to the Knob and on to Serpent Lake Trail.

Turn right (southwest) onto Trail #22, which is actually an old logging road here; the trail steepens as it steadily climbs the ridge through mixed-conifer vegetation to a large meadow, at about 2 miles. To the north, from where you've come, you can see the Gallegos Peak area, and to the south, the Jicarita Peak ridge. The trail skirts the west side of the meadow and soon reaches a junction

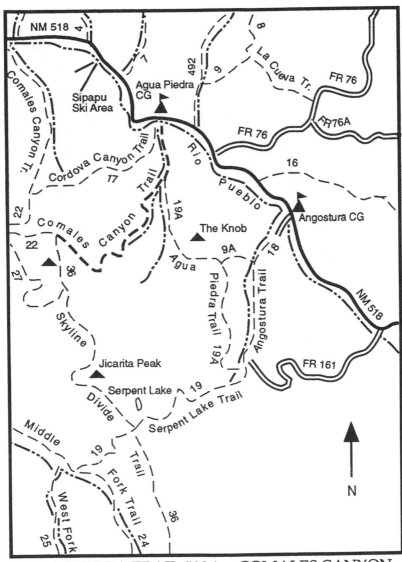

AGUA PIEDRA TRAIL #19A—COMALES CANYON
TRAIL #22

View to Ripley's Point

marked by a trail sign which indicates a turn more due west up the ridge (the sign says it's 4 miles to Jicarita Peak and 6 miles to Santa Barbara). The map shows that the trail also continues south and loops back to this clearing.

Comales Trail climbs steeply up the ridge to a switchback that turns sharply to your left. From here the trail continues climbing through the thick mixed-conifer vegetation for about a mile to a pond on your left called Esteros Tank. Past the pond the trail momentarily levels out, then climbs once again through more alpine-like vegetation to a great view; to the northeast you can see Gallegos Peak and on to the Angel Fire area; to the south Jicarita Peak ridge leads from Ripley's Point to Jicarita. It's a great place for lunch.

The trail continues a little farther to the junction with Skyline Divide Trail #36, which leads south to Ripley's Point and Jicarita Peak. Comales Trail #22 continues north along the ridge above the Rio Santa Barbara to its trailhead on NM 518. You can also access several trails that lead down to the Santa Barbara Campground road from Trail #22.

LA CUEVA CANYON TRAIL #492—LA CUEVA TRAIL #8—POTATO PATCH TRAIL #9

Length: 9 miles round trip
Degree of Difficulty: Moderate
Elevation: 8,500-10,200 feet
Maps: Trails Illustrated Carson National Forest; USGS Tres Ritos, Cerro Vista
Finding the Trailhead: From the junction of NM 518 and NM 75 (to Peñasco) follow 518 southeast 7.8 miles to the La Cueva Canyon trailhead on the north side of the highway, just as you enter the town of Tres Ritos. You'll have to find a place to park your vehicle alongside the highway, as there is no pull-off area.

These three trails can be hiked as a loop, beginning and ending at the La Cueva Canyon trailhead. La Cueva Canyon Trail leads 3^1/$_2$ miles up La Cueva Canyon where it junctions with La Cueva Trail. The loop follows La Cueva Trail down to La Cueva Lake, where Potato Patch Trail heads a mile west and ties back in with La Cueva Canyon Trail.

The trail heads north between several summer homes where a sign indicates that the trail is open to motorcycles. A trail sign says that it's 4 miles to La Cueva Peak (accessed off La Cueva Trail) and 5 miles to La Cueva Lake.

A short, steep climb follows the east side of La Cueva Creek before the trail swings around to the east, away from the creek. The terrain levels out in a stand of aspens, then continues northwest until the creek is within sight again.

At about a mile you enter a meadow area where an old cabin sits near the trail. A little farther into the meadow is the junction of Potato Patch Trail, to the right (east), our return route. Another old fallen-down cabin sits near this trail.

The trail crosses the creek to the west side. If you hike this trail in late spring or early summer you may have a hard time crossing the creek here, but just follow the creek until you can find a narrow spot or some logs leading across the water. Cinquefoil, buttercup, and candytuft (in the spring) are prolific. Continue through the trees to the junction of the newly rerouted trail, just before the old trail crosses the creek again. A sharp switchback heads up the hill to a great view of the Jicarita Peak ridge. The trail continues to climb the ridge to another long switchback. You'll pass a trick

La Cueva Lake

tank, where the trail levels out, then climbs again as it swings around to the east. A trail sign indicates a right turn along FT 492. Another trail marker guides you left at a junction with an old road, and soon you'll reach the junction with La Cueva Trail #8. Stay to the right (left leads to FR 442) and follow La Cueva Trail through a meadow to the canyon drainage where the old La Cueva Canyon Trails heads down the creek.

La Cueva Trail gently climbs to a meadow, crosses a creek, and levels out. There's a view here of the Jicarita Peak ridge, which you will continue to see as the trail descends the canyon. The trail passes through an aspen stand, then enters spruce-fir forest and comes into a meadow below La Cueva Peak. You can't see the peak from here, but if you continue along the trail you'll soon reach another meadow where a spur trail to the left (north) leads to La Cueva Peak. If you have time, you can follow this trail around to the backside of the peak and ascend to a panoramic view of the area.

La Cueva Trail continues down the canyon and reveals a sweeping view of both the Jicarita ridge and the east side of the Sangres. A sign at the bottom of the hill points straight ahead to

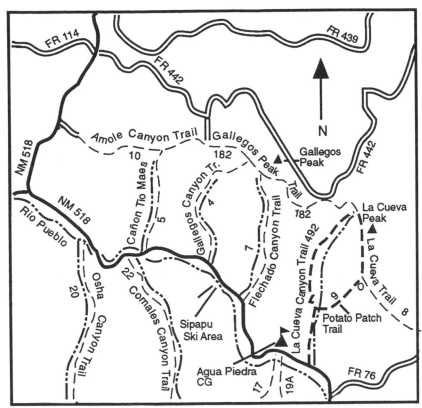

LA CUEVA CANYON TRAIL #492—LA CUEVA TRAIL #8—POTATO PATCH TRAIL #9 LOOP

La Cueva Lake and behind you to La Cueva Peak (an old trail leading northeast is visible here). The lake sits just below you in a large meadow and, when I was there in late May, had flooded a stand of aspen trees to the east. Follow a barely discernable trail around the lake to the right (west) and you'll see where it enters the trees again on the far side of the lake. You'll soon enter another meadow where a trail sign indicates the continuation of La Cueva Trail bearing southeast; look ahead and to your right and you'll see another trail sign. This sign indicates Potato Patch Trail, which leads 1 mile west back to La Cueva Canyon Trail #492. The view from this meadow extends south to the ridge and west towards the Peñasco area.

Follow Potato Patch Trail in a steep descent through thick spruce-fir forest to the junction with La Cueva Canyon Trail in the meadow next to the old cabin. Turn left (south) and follow the trail 1¹/₂ miles back to the trailhead in Tres Ritos.

AGUA PIEDRA TRAIL #19A—ANGOSTURA TRAIL #18 LOOP

Length: 8 miles round trip
Degree of Difficulty: Moderate
Elevation: 8,800-10,200 feet
Maps: Trails Illustrated Carson National Forest; USGS Tres Ritos, Jicarita Peak, Holman
Finding the Trailhead: From the junction of NM 518 and NM 75 (to Peñasco) follow 518 southeast for 10.8 miles to Angostura Campground. There is no sign marking the campground so be sure to watch carefully for the turnoff on the south side of the highway. To find the trailhead you can walk or drive the 1-mile primitive road that leads through the summer home area to a dead-end sign where the trail begins. A trail sign here says Angostura Trail #110, 493 (the trail through Alamitos Canyon): Serpent Lake, 8 miles; Santa Barbara Divide, 10 miles.

Santa Barbara Pole and Tie Company

The Santa Barbara Pole and Tie Company was founded by A. B. McGaffey to supply 16 million railroad ties to the Atchison, Topeka, and the Santa Fe. As William deBuys describes it in his book *Enchantment and Exploitation*, the reason the AT&SF needed these poles was to lay a second set of tracks across New Mexico and Arizona so the company could stay competitive with new shipping lines using the Panama Canal. McGaffey purchased 24,750 acres of the former Santa Barbara Land Grant and 41,000 acres of the Mora Land Grant.

During its years of operation, from 1909 to 1926, the Santa Barbara Pole and Tie Company was a ubiquitous presence in the high country below Jicarita Peak near the present day Pecos Wilder-

Burros hauling logs for Santa Barbara Pole and Tie Company

ness. Timber suitable for ties was cut all the way to timber line, and portable sawmills were constructed at elevations as high as eleven thousand feet. Wooden flumes, still visible today, carried the timbers down the mountain.

In order to mill the larger timbers McGaffey and his workers built a narrow-gauge railway up the side canyons of the Santa Barbara watershed, which connected the timber sites with a main sawmill (with a capacity of 1,000 ties a day) at the mouth of the canyon. To get the milled ties down to Embudo and the Rio Grande, workers stockpiled the ties along the Rio Pueblo and the Rio Santa Barbara until late April or early May, when the spring runoff carried these hundreds of thousands of ties down river. As deBuys explains to his incredulous readers, wondering how in the world the narrow Rio Pueblo and Rio Santa Barbara could carry all that timber, even during spring run-off, McGaffey's men built crib dams, which held the water until they were dynamited for the water's release. This engineering feat, like that of the Elizabethtown mining canals, has left its legacy all over these areas we now hike for recreation. It's hard to imagine the ingenuity and hard labor that created it. Unfortunately, we're also still dealing with the company's legacy of over-cut forests.

The Hike

This loop hike both begins and ends in Angostura Campground. The trail crosses Angostura Creek and heads up the canyon through lush vegetation. Just a few hundred yards up the trail a spur trail, #9A, turns sharply right (west). This is the route this loop hike takes to Agua Piedra Trail (Angostura Trail continues south, up the canyon, and will be hiked on the return leg of the loop).

Follow Trail #9A about three-fourths mile along the ridge, a steady ascent, to the meadow below Jicarita Ridge. You can just see the high peaks of the ridge, almost always spotted with snow, even in mid-summer. Trail #9A junctions with Agua Piedra Trail #19 in the middle of the meadow. To the right (north), it leads towards the Knob and on to its trailhead in Agua Piedra Campground. To the left (south), our route, it leads to Serpent Lake Trail and the junction with Angostura Trail at FR 161. There are a series of creeks throughout the meadow, making this a good camp site to take kids on a short backpack trip.

The trail levels out as it heads south through thick mixed-conifer vegetation. For the first mile the trail is wide and straightforward; it then makes a sharp turn to the left and climbs steeply uphill until it turns south again and reaches a meadow. Cross the meadow and on the south side of the meadow the trail becomes an old logging road, one of many in the area used years ago by the Santa Barbara Pole and Tie Company. The trail keeps climbing through several meadows, full of sebadillosos and elephant head, as it continues south. After more than 2 miles the trail divides; stay to the left, cross Angostura Creek, and one last uphill climb brings you to a junction. A blue arrow on a tree points out the continuation of Trail #19, now called Serpent Lake Trail, to the right (south); turn left and follow the wide path down along the creek to the junction with FR 161, which leads 4 miles east to NM 518. The Angostura trailhead is found here at the junction with FR 161; a sign says the trail number is #18.

Follow Angostura Trail north through the trees to a junction where a sign picturing a rider on a horse indicates the continua-

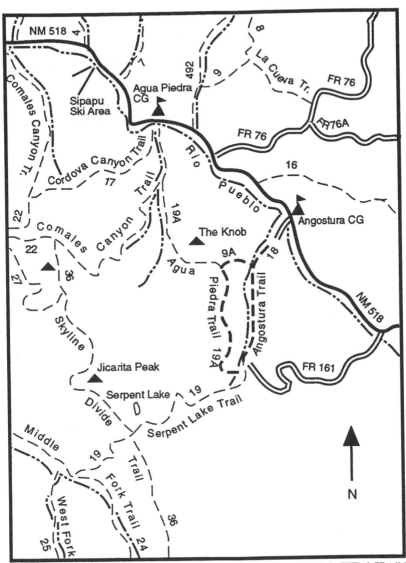

AGUA PIEDRA TRAIL #19A—ANGOSTURA TRAIL #18

tion of Angostura Trail to the left; Alamitos Canyon Trail turns right (east). It's a gentle descent along a wide forest path to a meadow where huge piles of weathered, stacked wood were left by the Santa Barbara Pole and Tie Company. Just past the meadow the trail starts following Angostura Creek, and the vegetation becomes lush—monkshood, cow parsnip, larkspur, and sky pilot color the trail. A small waterfall creates an inviting pool alongside the trail.

After several miles the trail moves farther away from the creek and passes through a thick stand of aspen trees, interspersed with small openings full of sebadillosos and checkermallow. The trail converges with the creek again as it approaches the trailhead. Continue past the junction with Trail #9A, our starting point, and return to your car at the dead end sign.

SERPENT LAKE TRAIL #19

Length: 8 miles round trip
Degree of Difficulty: Moderate
Elevation: 10,200-12,400 feet
Maps: Pecos Wilderness; Trails Illustrated Carson National Forest; USGS Jicarita Peak
Finding the Trailhead: From the junction of NM 518 and NM 75 (to Peñasco) follow 518 southeast for 13.7 miles to FR 161. Turn right (southwest) onto Forest Road 161 and follow this all-weather road 4 miles to where it's been birmed. From here, follow the road about a half mile to its termination at the trailhead. There's a sign here indicating the Angostura Trail, which heads north to Angostura Campground (described previously).

This trail lies partially within the Pecos Wilderness but is easily hiked in a day and is one of the most beautiful hikes in the Tres Ritos area. Serpent Lake trail heads west, up into the trees. This first part of the trail is an old four-wheel drive road, but it soon narrows to a trail. About 1/2 mile from the trailhead is the junction with Agua Piedra Trail #19A, which heads north to Agua Piedra Campground. Follow Trail #19 to the left (west) as it begins climbing to Serpent Lake. At about 3/4 mile, the trail crosses the Holman

Serpent Lake

irrigation ditch, then continues in a steady uphill climb to the switchbacks across the small meadows that define the terrain. Here you will find the bristlecone pine, one of the oldest trees growing in the Pecos. The climb to the wilderness boundary, at about $2^1/2$ miles, is fairly gradual, with occasional steep places.

Another half-mile climb brings you to a sign that marks the spur trail leading down to Serpent Lake, to the right (north). A short, steep trail takes you down to the lake (actually two small lakes) basin in its spectacular setting below the Jicarita Peak ridge. Gentians, rose crown, and elephant head fill the basin meadows.

If you have the time and the stamina you can climb back to Trail #19 and continue on to Jicarita Peak ridge. The views are worth the hike. Follow the trail south to a major switchback which leads to a view of the lakes below, as well as views east towards Mora and north to Taos. At tree line switchbacks continue to the top of the Jicarita Peak ridge which extends to Santa Barbara Divide. Here, North Fork Trail #36 heads south along the ridge to Skyline Trail #251 and north around Jicarita Peak to Ripley's Point. The view is spectacular: northwest over the three forks of

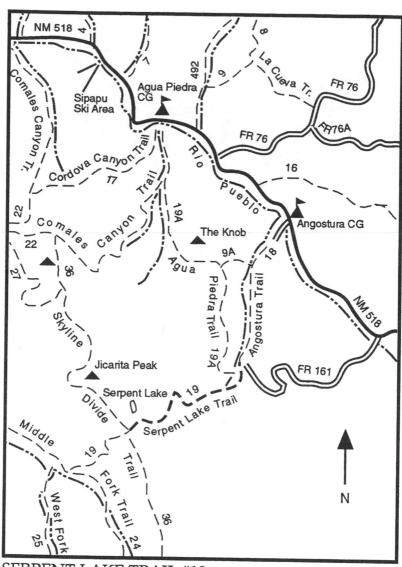

SERPENT LAKE TRAIL #19

the Rio Santa Barbara loom Chimayosos Peak, the Truchas Peaks, Sheep's Head Peak, and Trampas Peak.

Trail #19 continues west down a steep ascent (from 12,400 feet to just over 10,000 feet) to the junction of East Fork Santa Barbara Trail #26, which leads south to the Divide and north to Santa Barbara Campground.

```
┌─────────────────────────────────────────────────────┐
│                                                       │
│            Section IX. Santa Barbara                  │
│                                                       │
└─────────────────────────────────────────────────────┘
```

Santa Barbara Campground, near Peñasco, is one of the main entry points into the Pecos Wilderness. Several trails which lead into the country north of the wilderness area are accessed near the entrance to the campground. I've also included a description of West Fork Santa Barbara Trail, which leads into the wilderness, and can be followed for 3 or 4 miles for a lovely day hike.

INDIAN CREEK TRAIL #27
Length: 10 miles round trip
Degree of Difficulty: Moderate to Difficult
Elevation: 8,800-11,800 feet
Maps: Pecos Wilderness; Trails Illustrated Carson National Forest; USGS Jicarita Peak
Finding the Trailhead: Follow NM 73 south from Peñasco (the sign at the junction with NM 75 says NM 73 leads to Llano) to the turn left (east) onto Forest Road 116. Follow FR 116 6 miles to the wilderness parking lot at the campground; a sign indicates the Indian Creek trailhead just before the parking lot next to the turn-off to the lower Santa Barbara Campground. The sign says it's 5 miles to the Santa Barbara Divide and 8 miles to Jicarita Peak.

Indian Creek Trail leads from Santa Barbara Campground to Ripley's Point on Skyline Divide Trail. There is no established river crossing here, so you'll have to take your shoes off and wade across. Look for the blue marker on a tree indicating the start of the trail on the far side of the Rio Santa Barbara; the trail is periodically marked with these blazes as part of the National Recreation Trail system. You'll have to cross another small tributary, then cross Indian Creek to the south side of the canyon and pass through a gate.

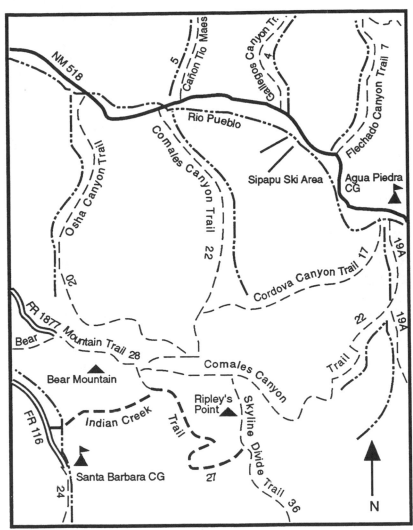

INDIAN CREEK TRAIL #27

The trail climbs moderately through thick vegetation to a large meadow ringed with aspen trees; aspens proliferate throughout the hike, making this a good one for the fall. You'll cross the creek to the north side and climb more steeply to another clearing

Indian Creek Trail

where the trail turns sharply away from the creek to the left (north). Someone has built an arrow of rocks indicating the turn. The trail enters a stand of aspen and leads to an expansive view south up the Rio Santa Barbara to the Truchas Peaks. Golden pea, lousewort, and strawberries line the trail.

It's about 2 miles to the top of the ridge, where a sign indicates the continuation of Indian Creek Trail to the right (south). To the left (north), the trail continues to Bear Mountain and junctions with Comales Canyon Trail #22, which can be used on a loop route. Follow Indian Creek Trail to the right, along the ridge, in a level hike through mixed-conifer forest. Soon the trail steepens again as it climbs towards the head of Indian Creek Canyon, where you'll cross the headwaters of Indian Creek. A view to the south extends all the way to the Pedernal in the Jemez Mountains; Bear Mountain is visible to the southwest. A pile of scrap planks indicates the former presence of the Santa Barbara Pole and Tie Company.

Once across the creek, you'll continue to climb across some scree to a switchback, marked with a blue blaze, indicating a turn left (east) as the trail heads up towards the Divide. The terrain is steeper here as the trail crosses numerous small creeks and spur trails until it heads into the rocky terrain below the Divide. There can be some confusion here as various routes climb up to the ridge, but if you stay on the most traveled route you'll reach the top of the ridge in a small grove of trees. Indian Creek Trail meets Skyline Divide Trail #36 on the ridge, just south of Ripley's Point. There is an expansive view north over the Agua Piedra drainage. To the right (south), Trail #36 continues 2 miles to Jicarita Peak. To the left (north), the trail leads to Ripley's Point and the junction with Comales Trail #22. This hike, combined with the following Indian Creek—Comales Trail route, can be hiked as a 10-mile loop, both beginning and ending at Santa Barbara Campground.

INDIAN CREEK TRAIL #27—COMALES CANYON TRAIL #22

Length: 8 miles round trip
Degree of Difficulty: Moderate
Elevation: 8,800-11,400 feet
Maps: Pecos Wilderness; Trails Illustrated Carson National Forest; USGS Jicarita Peak
Finding the Trailhead: Follow NM 73 south from Peñasco (the sign at the junction with NM 75 says NM 73 leads to Llano) to the turn left (east) onto Forest Road 116. Follow FR 116 6 miles to the

wilderness parking lot at the campground; a sign indicates the Indian Creek trailhead just before the parking lot next to the turn-off to the lower Santa Barbara picnic area. The sign says it's 5 miles to the Santa Barbara Divide and 8 miles to Jicarita Peak.

This hike begins along Indian Creek Trail, described in the previous section, then ties in with Comales Canyon Trail and continues to Skyline Divide Trail, north of Ripley's Point. It can be hiked as a 10-mile loop route with Indian Creek Trail.

Climb Indian Creek Trail to the sign which indicates the turn right, at the top of the ridge (2 miles). Instead of turning right (south), turn left (north), as if you were headed toward Bear Mountain. The trail follows a level route through aspen stands to a fenceline and gate, where one of the best views you'll ever have of the high Pecos Peaks spreads out before you to the southwest; you can see the entire Rio Santa Barbara watershed stretching from Jicarita Peak on Santa Barbara Divide, across the Truchas Peaks, and west to the San Leonardo ridge.

Turn north through the gate, and just a short distance along the level trail the route divides; to the left (northwest) the trail continues to Bear Mountain; to the right (east) the trail reaches a sign which indicates this is Comales Canyon Trail #22, leading 6 miles north to the Rio Pueblo on NM 518. Comales Canyon Trail climbs along a rocky route and periodically splits and merges; stay to the right at each turn in the trail. You'll reach a large meadow after about 1 mile, an obvious campsite with established fire rings. Here there's a view west to Bear Mountain and the village of Peñasco. Comales Canyon Trail continues left (east) across the meadow and continues climbing one half mile to a junction; Comales Canyon Trail continues left to its trailhead on NM 518; our route continues right, about one fourth mile, to a gate and sign indicating the continuation of Comales Canyon Trail to the right to Santa Barbara Divide. Continue a few feet along the now level trail to another sign at the junction with the Skyline Divide Trail #36, which continues right to Ripley's Point, and to the left the continuation of Comales Trail #22 to Agua Piedra Campground, 8 miles. If you follow Comales Trail down toward Agua Piedra just a few hundred yards there's a great view north towards Angel Fire and south along the Divide to Jicarita Peak.

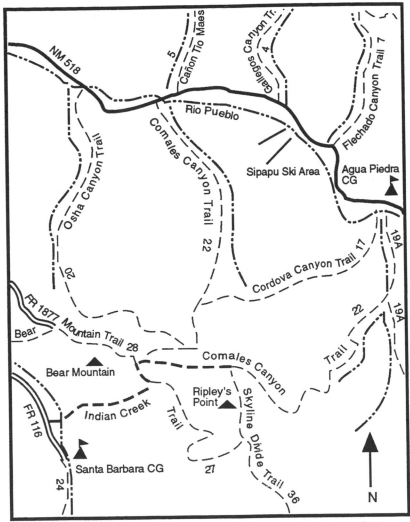

INDIAN CREEK TRAIL #27—COMALES CANYON
TRAIL #22

You can return the way you came or continue along Skyline
Divide Trail #36 to Ripley's Point and the junction with Indian
Creek Trail (about 1 mile), which leads back down to Santa Bar-

bara Campground (the entire loop is about 10 miles).

WEST FORK SANTA BARBARA TRAIL #24
Length: Variable mileage
Degree of Difficulty: Easy
Elevation: 8,800-10,000 feet
Maps: Pecos Wilderness; Trails Illustrated Carson National Forest; USGS Jicarita Peak, El Valle
Finding the Trailhead: Follow NM 73 south from Peñasco (the sign at the junction with NM 75 says NM 73 leads to Llano) to the turn left (east) onto Forest Road 116. Follow FR 116 6 miles to the wilderness parking lot at Santa Barbara Campground. Walk down the campground road to the southeast corner of the campground, where the trail heads south through a gate alongside the river.

This trail is within the Pecos Wilderness and is described in my book, *Hiking the Wilderness*. Accessed from Santa Barbara Campground, it follows the west fork of the Rio Santa Barbara all the way to the Santa Barbara Divide, 12 miles in length. A good day hike of about 3 or 4 miles leads to the meadows along the river where views extend south to Chimayosos Peak and the Divide. The trail follows the west side of the river in an easy climb through aspen forests. Gooseberry, raspberry, and strawberry proliferate along the trail. You'll pass the junction with Centennial Trail a short distance up the trail, and about 1 mile in is a sign indicating this is West Fort Trail #25, with distances of 10 miles to the Santa Barbara Divide (the north-south ridge that separates the Santa Barbara and Pecos watersheds) and 14 miles to Pecos Falls (via Middle Fork Trail).

About one half mile up the canyon, the trail crosses the river and continues to climb to the junction with the West and Middle Fork Trails, at about 2 miles. The sign says Pecos Falls to your left (east) along Middle Fork Trail #24, and the Santa Barbara Divide and Truchas Lakes straight ahead on West Fork Trail #25. Follow #25 as it traverses a small meadow, then crosses the middle fork of the Rio Santa Barbara (the west fork of the river is still on your right).

The trail soon begins its long, gentle ascent through the mead-

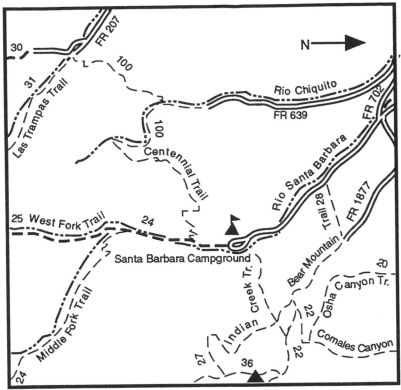

WEST FORK SANTA BARBARA TRAIL #24

ows that dominate the terrain, full of tulip gentians, sebadillosos, and cinquefoil. Aspens line the canyon walls, the sounds of the river accompany you on your walk, and Chimayosos Peak looms ahead, marking the divide.

After several miles of meadow, the trail crosses the West Fork Rio Santa Barbara to the west side of the canyon. This is probably about as far as you'll want to travel on a day hike. The return trip offers a whole new perspective on your hike—it always looks completely different going down

BIBLIOGRAPHY

Barker, Elliott. *Beatty's Cabin*. Albuquerque: University of New Mexico Press, 1953.

Barker, Elliott. *When the Dogs Bark 'Treed'*. Albuquerque: University of New Mexico Press, 1946.

deBuys, William. *Enchantment and Exploitation*. Albuquerque: University of New Mexico Press, 1985.

Julyan, Robert. *The Place Names of New Mexico*. Albuquerque: University of New Mexico Press, 1996.

Pearson, Jim Berry. *The Red River—Twining Area: A New Mexico Mining Story*. Albuquerque: University of New Mexico Press, 1986.

Photo credits: Thanks to Betty Brown, pages 21 and 65; Roy Barker, page 39; Jan Pfeiffer, page 56; U. S. Forest Service, page 91.